*Dedicated to my parents:*
*Constant Georges MERITZA*
*(1929-2011)*
*Josiane MERITZA*
*(1936-)*
*and to the one who shares my life*
*my partner Sophie*

***Special thanks :***

Yoann MERITZA

# The lead of life

*Éditeur:*

*BoD-Books on Demand,*

*12/14 rond point des Champs Élysées*

*75008 Paris, France*

*Printing: BoD-Books on Demand, Norderstedt, Germany*

*legal deposit April 2020*

*ISBN: 9782322202676*

*cover picture :*

*license: cco 1.0 universal / (cco 1.0)*

*graphics: Yoann MERITZA*

*The lead of life*

*Original french title : « L'ami de l'âme »*

*Copyright 00067599-1- © Yoann MERITZA*

*December 2019 - rights reserved*

*I can't remember how it all started*

*I don't remember if it was a dream or reality*

*Or even how many years had passed*

*Was I lost in my thoughts looking for the truth?*

*In this silence of the mind, I find my destiny*

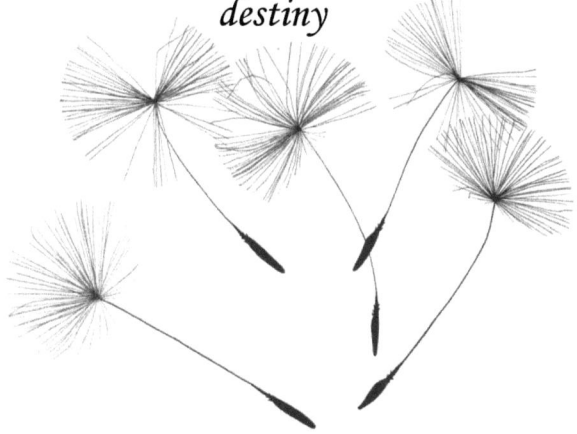

# A FEW WORDS ABOUT THE AUTHOR

Yoann MERITZA is a coach and an essay writer specializing in personal development.
He is also the author of the bestseller "How to reprogram your subconscious mind ?"

He was born on March 28, 1978 in Bonneville in Haute-Savoie and grew up in Cluses in the same department. He studied accounting and trained as an SME-SMI collaborator where he learned NLP (Neurolinguistic Programming). He has participated in numerous internships and seminars on communication and is passionate about personal development. Self-taught at heart, he continues to perfect himself in communication and the study of human nature by following in the footsteps of many authors of the same theme such as Napoleon Hill, Norman Vincent Peal, Florence Scovel Shinn or Doctor Joseph Murphy.

He creates his own method by synthesizing from his many readings on the subject and brings readers to a broad understanding of the field of personal growth by a simplified approach for assimilation at all levels, his concern being always the precision of the theme chosen and to provide novice readers with clear and affordable answers at all cultural levels.

Son of a veteran and former soldier, he is also a member of the 27ème BCA and UNC-Alpes friendship.

## *Foreword*

Hello to all reader friends,

I know ! Another book on personal development, but believe it or not, this one is totally different from the others, because it has an appeal both spiritual and extraordinary, and you will understand over the pages why I express myself thus .

"The lead of life" is a work like its content. It is not written like the others which are pre-formatted with chapters and parts, and they are divided into "titles", « acts », and "stages". It will invite you through fictional stories that anyone can create, if you are inspired and creative enough.

You may be a little lost at first, but this is voluntary. Disturbing and captivating, welcome to the world as I see it, a world where reality and imagination meet, madness and reason.

Specializing in the subject of human nature, I explain to you the whole mechanism of what constitutes what one might call "the inner world".

Each author has, of course, his own methods to explain it, but here is a new one that will certainly surprise you, shock you at first, but with a bit of hindsight, and thinking well, over this strange adventure that you are going to live, you will finally know the true deep nature of the human, and challenge a little everything you have learned so far.

"The lead of life" opens up a new extension of the possibilities of the spirit which goes far beyond what I could call "conventions" (I'll explain this to you later).

After reading this, you will no longer trust what you will see, hear, or believe. This is not brainwashing, others have done it for me. You are already the victims of a functioning system which is not in accord with your inner being.

"The lead of life!", will give you to think, to react, even if its content may seem controversial, there will be funds of truths that I would like you to exploit.

As I keep saying, beware of appearances, and knowing the causes, you have a real plan that will help you discover more than just reading.

In a pretty case, there is a diamond, and you almost have it in your hand, but before that, there is still a long way to go and follow the directions. I'm not saying it will be easy, but it only takes a simple lantern to light your way in search of the precious, it's the path to a very great legacy that awaits you for those who are perceptive.

I would just ask you one thing, it is to have a very open mind, and you will discover that the world in which you live is not what you believe, you will better distinguish the false from the true and you will be able to make your own choices about what happens next in your life.

I wish you all a good read, and also that your conscience finally opens.

Best regards,

Yoann MERITZA
Specialist author

\*\*

*Rule n°1*

*To get noticed, do something different!*

\*\*

# Act I
# The spirit

CE N'EST PAS PARCE QUE
TU AS RAISON, QUE MOI J'AI TORT.
C'EST JUSTE QUE TU N'AS PAS
LE MÊME POINT DE VUE QUE MOI.

« *It's not because you've right that i've wrong. It's just because we've not the same point of view.* »

## *The epilogue*

*The night fell on Paris, and I remember my arrival this day by train, I had made a very long trip, but it is not of this that I will tell you about, but I will come back to it later, or unless your keen senses understand it quickly enough.*

*The station was crowded, travelers jostling in a deafening din. I was a few minutes from my meeting, maybe I had made this trip, in the fold of a disturbing silence.*

*There were soldiers everywhere, accusing eyes accompanied by dogs strangling in their collars, and leading their master in rhythm. Fear of a terrorist attack was still ubiquitous in people's minds.*

*My watch said 2:26 pm and I told myself that it was impossible to be on time, making my way between the crowd, I finally arrived at the exit of this station and that I had to run.*

*What other choice did I have? Plus it was raining heavily, and I only had my suit and my Gazette in my hand. Razing the walls and desperately looking for shelter, my soaked diary fell to shreds on the floor.*

*But finally, I arrived at my destination, that famous bar that my friend told me about, I push the door in the ringing of a rather archaic bell. It was enough with this single sound for all the heads turn away, the people in this bar gave the feeling of feeling guilty.*

*My simple hello echoed as in an exhibition of statues with frozen and lost eyes, would it be the alcohol that had soaked them?*

*I didn't have time to sit down when the bar owner asked me what I wanted to drink, and barely ordered two coffees when my friend arrived at the bar. The meeting ended in apology for being late, when I thought the opposite, but was justified by the presence of police and soldiers who search everyone on the street, for fear of a new terrorist attack.*

*A few days earlier, an office had exploded in the center of the city, carrying in his ashes four important personalities, and it must be said that it was rather tense at the moment.*

*For a long time, we had discussed about a book, and it must be said that between authors, discussions often revolved around these subjects, but also about the news, because we too have a daily life.*

*He took a pocket full of manuscripts from his satchel and handed it to me, and I asked him what it was. As "The Epilogue" emptied (it was the name of this Parisian bar), a strange calm invaded this rather tense place.*

*He told me he was on a new project and he wanted my participation to finish it, a collaboration between two authors, but I was not very accommodating to accept his request for the simple reason that I often work alone.*

*Then he said to me:*

*"Yoann, we've known each other for a long time now!" I know we've lost touch for a very long time, and now that you're awakening to a new day in your life, I'd like to join you in continuing to write this book."*

*The concept that he presented to me was the following, he would like to create a fantastic story around my favorite field, personal development.*

*I replied:*

*"Dear friend, I fully appreciate your enthusiasm and your desire to want to make a book together. I appreciate that you have thought of me, but give me time to think about it."*

*With these words, he handed me an incomplete manuscript that ended on page 21, titled "The lead of life"*

*Why was he giving me something untoward? So that I can finish the story.*

*I took the manuscript and put it in my jacket pocket, the weather was changing, in both senses of the word because there was excitement outside and it was not advisable to go out now, despite a thinned time.*

*Suddenly, a crash made me jump, it was one of the panes of "The Epilogue" which had just exploded under the effect of a projectile. Gunshots and screams were getting louder, and many will tell me that we are living in a funny time ...... funny ....... I don't think that's the right word, I would say it was pretty hard to feel threatened by an attack at any time, and times were tough in this fall 1943 season.*

Some will wonder how I landed at that time, and I will answer them that it is thanks to an event which occurred a little further in this text, but do not look! You will not find it presented here, because like all history, everything has a beginning, and it is not at the beginning of this book.

Let me tell you a fabulous story, a universe halfway between the real and the imaginary, filled with magic, that which is found in each of us.

For a long time I asked myself "How was I going to write such a book? ", And it's not my habit to tell a fantastic story by combining personal development, and I wanted to make it something fun, impacting your mind.

So, I say to all of you "welcome to my world! ", That of the possible, which gives you the power to be who you want and when you want.

As I said, this book is on the borderline between the real and the imaginary and invites you to become a child again for a moment.

Forget what you have learned so far and let yourself embark on this wonderful fantastic journey mixing the rational and the confusing.

And if you have been disturbed by my vivid imagination, this lets you predict the future.

Our way of thinking comes from a succession of images that have paraded in our life, there is a form of neuro-association between a word, a form, an event, and the information which are linked to this I come to quote, such as "the Epilogue" which was only a title and the name of a bar, which you quite naturally associated with "the end of a book" and the year of my history which turned upside down all the context, which you believed to be related to the current events related to the publication of this book, but also elements which you obscured from the start, and which you will understand subsequently, I hope for you, including the name of my friend that you all know, although it may surprise you, as it is common.

"The lead of life" takes all its flavor in the imagination, and basically, what is the imagination? But yet, and despite appearances, it is indeed personal development (in another form I understand it). I would describe it as something very "spiritual", "subtle", "deep", never trust appearances!

Your intellect will be put to the test in this treasure hunt, the main hero of which is not what you think, and all I can tell you is that he is much closer to you than you cannot imagine.

Finally, you will find answers to your questions, and one in particular, if you are discerning:

"Who are you really?" "

I'll let you meditate on it, between the lines, and never forget this essential rule:

"Never trust appearances! They are deceptive!" "

# *"Viatorem"*

What you are about to discover now comes from a true story, and even if everything will seem impossible to you, it really happened, and I hope that your keen minds will understand the course and the purpose of it. It happened a very long time ago, but when I say this, it seems quite relative, you will understand why a little further.

*This story is a great mystery that no one to date has been able to solve. It was first told in 1984 by François' grandson.*

*The adventure, like all those of the same kind, began in April 1897 near Verdun where a young man was playing with his little brother. These two fair-haired heads were running through the cornfields, even though their father had forbidden them to go.*

*Suddenly, the youngest disappeared so quickly that the elder, did not even have time to turn around, just the reflex to do so after the sound of the ground creaking, smothered by the leaves of the corn. What had happened? In an instant, the younger son found himself a floor lower after the ground, and his crying alerted the larger of the two.*

*He rushed into what appeared to be an underground gallery or a secret hideout, and there were stacks of cases filled with old manuscripts with rather strange inscriptions.*

*"Come help me, I'm afraid! Said the youngest.*

*" Do not worry ! Hold out ! I'm going to get help! Replied the other.*

*In large strides, he ran to the family home, and in no time, he was at the entrance, completely breathless. He entered the main room where their father was, a tough man, of good education, strengthened by the work in the fields and to whom nothing is more afraid. He was reading a book, his glasses resting on the tip of his nose, sitting on his brown velvet armchair.*

*He looked at his older son and asked the following question:*

*P "Hey baby, you're very pale, what's happening to you?"*

*then the son replied with a short breath:*

*F "It is ... it is ... .. Henry .."*

*P "Who has he with Your younger brother? Have you argued yet?"*

*F "No ... ... this is not .... This is ... .."*

*P "Finally François, make understandable sentences, because even my ears have trouble recomposing what you are trying to tell me!"*

*F "It's Henry ... .. he is ... ... he fell in a hole"*

P "What do you mean?" Explain yourself more clearly!"

F "It is … ..in a hole … … in the field"

The father sighed, and like an old man, he leaned on the armrests of his armchair and with a rather lively air, he lectured his son:

P "Damn it, but how many times should I tell you? I strictly forbade you to go play in the cornfields, and this is what happens when you don't listen to me! You don't know what dangers you run!"

F "But papa! I ….."

P "Just tell me where Henry is, I don't want to know anything else, and we'll talk about the sanctions later, meanwhile, show me where he fell!""

*On these words, the father took a rope and two oil lamps and with his son, went to the field where Henry had disappeared.*

*The ground to cover was immense, and François could not remember more precisely where he and his younger brother had lost sight of each other.*

*The night came with calls:*

*"HENRY …… .HENRY …… WHERE ARE YOU?""*

*Suddenly a distant sound was heard! it was Henry!*

*H "I'm here dad! "*

*Pierre (that was the name of the father of the two children) came running until the screams got louder and louder.*

*He found the hole where Henry had fallen, and slowly approaching this cavity, he lit the bottom and saw his youngest, curled up on himself, scared and trembling! Henry looked up and exclaimed:*

*H "I thought you would never find me! "*

*P "We're here! Hold on my dear! "*

*At these words, the older brother brought the rope while his father lit up this rather sinister place.*

*P "Come down kid while I hold the rope!" "*

*François wrapped the rope around his waist and began to descend into this underground room. Then joined his little brother.*

*F "How are you Henry? Nothing broken ? "*

*H "No, but I was so scared! There is something wrong with this place! "*

*On these words, François explored this cavity. There were the cases mentioned above, but also, they had inscriptions in German, artillery pieces, rifles and helmets, and this environment seemed foreign to the two young aspiring explorers.*

*In a small box placed above these boxes, there were letters written in German.*

*Their father, hearing nothing more, exclaimed:*

*P "Are you okay?" Why do you take so long to go up? It's getting late ! Come back up right away! "*

*F "Everything is fine! Just that ... wait a few minutes, we are coming! "*

*As he said these words, François lit up a corner of the room, and what he saw made him cold in the back. There was an inscription on the wall, as written in blood letters.*

*F "Dad! Do you know what "Vorsicht vor dem Reisenden!" Means? "*

*P "It's German! At least what I remember from the War of 70 (Franco-Prussian conflict), that means "beware of the traveler", now go back up! You scare me now and I don't want to get angry! "*

*After these few words, he said to himself:*

*"Damn, I'm going to go get them!"*

*and he went down to join them.*

*And there it was astonishment! He recognized an old military hiding place, but something was wrong with the context, because there were mash press sticks in these cases, and it was more and more mysterious, but he was still a thousand miles from suspect what was to follow.*

P *"My children! You made me one of those scares, I was getting impatient upstairs! And what is this place?"*

F *"We thought you would know"*

*On closer inspection, their father took one of the letters written in German which were in a box. It was a love letter from what he translated.*

*This former soldier had had plenty of time to hear German words during the War of 70, and he was able to translate its content:*

*" My beloved; I put these few words on this sheet, and I find it hard to write them! My frostbite makes me suffer, I barely have the strength to continue and I have so much to tell you!*

*I am also afraid that the censor will prevent me from telling you under what conditions I live, and I so much want to brave the prohibitions, very want to hug you, want to flee this hell to join you. I would like to spend the end of the year holidays with you my love. We are all waiting, my comrades and I, for the end of this conflict, so much brutality, so much screaming and suffering, how can two nations manage to tear each other apart? How do governments come to prohibit a crime against their people, but allow it against another? it's a real carnage and I'm afraid, afraid of losing you forever. I'm not even sure I'm going to finish 1916 even though we're only a few days away, and it would be wonderful if... .. "*

*P "1916 ????? Shouted Pierre.*

*This place was nothing normal, how was it possible that a letter written almost 20 years later ended up in the hands of this solid man?*

*It shattered his beliefs, he was amazed! So much that he forgot that he had to go up, him and his children, because night had fallen, and there was almost no oil left, but still took the time to take this box full of letters before to reach the surface, and to mark with a stake the precise place of their discovery.*

*Returning to their home, the father took his children to bed. That night, everything was calm, and he had forgotten to sermonize them for having broken his prohibitions.*

*He went to his bedroom, he looked at the contents of the box he had found earlier in this underground room. No longer seeing the passage of time and no longer finding sleep, shocked by what he had discovered, he peeled several letters, and at the bottom of this box, there was something, a kind of double bottom.*

*So, curious to find out what was underneath, he took his knife, and with the blade, opened this double bottom, and what was behind was a book called "Viatorem".*

While leafing through this book, he was surprised to find that it was in French, but the author was unknown to him, even though the Germans held it, and he discovered an incredible story, at least for the context of the time.

What I can tell you about what he discovered, friends of readers, is a part of this book ending with "…. beware of appearances, they are not what they seem! ", but even more curious, is that this book seemed to cross the years, it was shaken by what it had discovered in it, but the tiredness won and he wanted to go to rest. It must also be said that it was already 11 p.m. and that his children had been sleeping for a while.

Pierre put the book in the box on the bedside table, open on the last page he had read before going to lie down on his bed as he was dressed.

*The next day, Pierre was awakened by a strange sound he did not know, it was stunning. He no longer recognized anything about his room, the walls were covered with sky blue colored paper which seemed to make the room ugly, and also realized that it was not his bed, the colors of which contrasted with his costume. of wool.*

*His box found the day before had disappeared, as well as all the furniture, there was instead rather strange furniture in colors that he did not know, then, approached a curious black box, with buttons and numbers, there was a screen, and this box was made of an unknown material, but that's where the sound came from. This object seemed to move by means of vibrations at the same time as a sort of bizzare music sang its song.*

*P "What the hell is this witchcraft?" "*

*He was also surprised that a child receiving his Christmas present observed the object for a long time before looking around.*

*Everything he owned had disappeared from his room, and it was filled with things he didn't know.*

*Then he tried to call his children, but no answer came to his ears. But what he didn't know was that the house was not that empty.*

*On the floor below, there was a couple with their children, and they froze on the spot, at breakfast time. They heard a stranger screaming in a loud voice.*

*Pierre, intrigued by this silence, descended, vomiting:*

*"Damn it, what's going on here, and why is no one answering me?"*

*On these words and going down the stairs, he had the same surprise as the other inhabitants of this place.*

*What happened next has been kept secret until this day, so there is no written or video record of these events. All that remains of this story has been passed on by word of mouth.*

*According to Sylvie, 46 years old today, a man, in period attire, had entered their home, it was in 2007. They called the police and the individual was taken away for breach of domicile.*

*the man in question refrained from saying that he was at home and that his name was Pierre Dumont. But all he has gathered is that he has been recognized as insane and interned, and to this day, now 54 years old, he still claims that he comes from another era and that his name is Pierre Dumont.*

*Unfortunately, there is no longer any evidence of who he really was. No identity document, no branded clothing, no clue, it's as if it never existed. Just what he had on him, a black wool suit, a matching waistcoat, a white shirt and shoes made of leather.*

*François' grandson, Pierre's son, died of cancer in 2003, but he knew this mysterious story of disappearance. And it was his wife, Myriam, who told me his story, albeit suspicious.*

*The place where Henry fell was never found, and years have passed. And in the meantime, you know, there were two conflicts in 1914-1918 and in 1939-1945. The cornfield did not survive the first bombings of the First World War, transforming this vast area into a heap of clay. Times were difficult for Pierre's family, leaving two orphaned children, no longer having a mother, because she had died a few years earlier from a very long illness.*

*Shortly after, François and Henry were taken care of by their uncle, who settled with them in the house, and resumed farming, which continued until the first dark hours that the country was going to know.*

*The land, after the conflicts, was abandoned, it became difficult to cultivate something on it. Today we can see weeds, brambles, or nettles that have taken possession of this irregular surface, the bombs having shaped it.*

*For his part, Pierre, under the effect of the drugs, shakes his head back and forth and continues to mumble sentences without tail or head:*

*"I was in this book! I was there from the start ... ... I was still there! up to page 43............... ..; ...... .Viatorem ............ ... The epilogue ...... .The lead of life... ..... it's not normal that!... ... Viatorem! "*

*I can never say it enough in this book, beware of appearances, they are not what they seem!*

Thinking is not really your own, it reacts by processing information in positive and negative, just like a computer program that uses binary code, even if its functioning is not quite the same. She takes information, analyzes and processes it according to her neuro-associative understanding.

Thought accepts or rejects information, depending on the information from your paradigm.

For example, imagine that you are in a group of friends, it asks you if you will accept such or such individuals to join it, so there is a constraint in relation to the image you want to give.

In the strictest sense, it must be said that this group of friends is very hard and that they do not tolerate that you think differently from them, but you would do everything to stay with them, even if it is a question of making suffer, or become selective in relation to this or these individuals wishing to join the group.

And that's where it all comes into play, and I'm going through that process. This is very subtle in appearance, because if you follow the thoughts of your friends, you are not free from your own, and yet, in everyday life, you are a follower. Ask yourself, why are you making this or that choice, is it of your own free will and mindfulness, or are you being forced a little bit to follow community standards? In a way, you make an unconscious choice, that of following others that you forget to be yourself, with its differences and its extravagances.

The reality is this, you don't follow your own thought, and you just have the illusion of it, and you are in a system belonging to the collective consciousness and you do not accept your deep nature, your extravagance, by fear of rejection or mockery.

What if being different was your true nature? Instead of following the dictate of the mass effect. So ask yourself why you like certain things and others not, is it really your choice?

Is that why I cannot stress it enough when I tell you never to trust appearances, they are not what they appear to be, and what do you really believe is what you want?

If for the moment the story has no meaning, it will have if you follow the pages of this book, just let the elements fall into place!

**

*Rule n°2*

*Never trust appearances*

**

## *the flea market*

*You are probably wondering how did I know Myriam?*

*It was a few years ago, during a flea market. I was bargain-hunting from stand to stand, watching uninspiring trinkets. There were vases, records, paintings, toys, and all the other junk that few people would burden themselves with.*

*However, my attention was drawn to an old book. It was out of age, worn, damaged, and the leaf cornices had become rounded. Taking it in my hands, it seemed to fall apart, the binding was detached from the pages that had lost their freshness, and everything had to be restored.*

*Curiously also, the name of the author of this book was identical to mine, internally, I was proud to say to myself "I am the author of this book (jokingly said!), And I thought that it* would be interesting to restore it, because I like to tell stories and this one was interesting, she spoke, of what I could decipher of it of a strange character who was called "Viatorem" (like the Title of the book).

From what I know, having forced my eyes to the characters discolored by time, he is a traveler who knows neither time nor space who finds refuge in being and who creates alternative realities.

For him, the imaginary and the real do not exist, but he nevertheless makes the junction between the two.

"Viatorem" is a truest character, I can guarantee you, even if you don't believe me yet, but it will come! You will come to ask yourself the following question:

"Is everything in this book reality, and am I just an imagination?" "

*Let me tell you this:*

*Perhaps you are not part of this world, and you are nothing more than a character in a book! And right now, someone is reading your adventures!*

*You may have the feeling of being real, of moving, of breathing, but it is possible that you are only the creation of a spirit which gives you the impression of evolving in your reality.*

*Perhaps the same thing will happen to you as Peter, a power is present in this book, and you will wake up, you will see a new place, in another era, but for the moment, what you are experiencing is only an illusion of your mind. But maybe it will be this new place that will be another illusion.*

*The problem in your so-called reality is that you accepted it as such, sitting on your chair, your armchair or your sofa, under a tree or leaning against a wall, there are even some who flip through the pages of this mysterious book in a shop, and I tell you "It is not good! Rest this book or buy it! "*

*This is what the stand saleswoman said to me who saw me taking the book and who then said to me "if you take it, it will only cost you 10 €".*

*Interested, I asked her where she had gotten this book.*

*The saleswoman told me a funny story, this book belonged to her deceased husband, he had inherited it from his father, who himself had it from his father François.*

*She told me an amazing story, that of a family that had experienced a great misfortune.*

*You know the beginning of this story that I told you a little earlier, but what happened next will freeze your blood.*

*On this morning in April 1897, two brothers woke up in a disturbing calm, their father did not call them, he who usually grumbled after them to get up.*

*There was deadly silence, only the ticking of a pendulum was free to express itself.*

*Worried, the two children went to their father's room, but he was not there!*

*On the bedside table, in a box, was an open book on page 43 which told a more than extraordinary story, that of a man with the same name as their father, who woke up in the future. But looking at the pages back, they were shocked! They closed the book because it was about these two brothers and their father, everything was there! The cornfield, the underground cavity, everything was mentioned as they lived it.*

*They wanted to keep the secret of this event, because they found this book too dangerous and have never been further in the text, imagining a form of witchcraft inside.*

*What one of them did, however, was write a letter to people who would live in the house in the future, and put it in a safe place, free from the ravages of time, that's what he believed, because to date, the letter has never arrived at its destination.*

*The box had been stored in the attic with the book inside, but the letters were destroyed because, what's the point of keeping mail in German?*

*The story was passed down from generation to generation, like a family heirloom, and the book ended up on a stand in a flea market.*

*Why was she selling it? Simply because, like many families, she wanted to make ends meet during this period, and what was more, there were too many painful memories related to her deceased spouse. Anyway, he was ruined, and keeping this in his apartment was very unhealthy, having taken mold from the cover. She was nervous and didn't even have animals in her house!*

*How did she end up in an apartment? Shortly after the death of her husband, she was already experiencing financial difficulties, and that the only way for her to get out of it was to put her husband's house up for sale.*

*the agricultural activity of the family estate did not bring luck either to Pierre's children or to the rest of the generations, the corn was no longer growing, the land had become incultivable, as if it were in bad luck. Two wars had passed there, drawing furrows of blood and suffering.*

*Pierre's family hung on to the end to keep the estate, they did it by the sweat of their brow, finding other jobs as farm workers. But the events were not as we would like them, the ground was abandoned. it had become a mass grave due to the events that everyone does not forget.*

*This explains why the letter from François intended for the future owners was never found, because not only was it in a secret place, and all those of the family were aware of this mail, but, by the force of things and thinking to stay long until 2007 (date cited in the book "Viatorem"), it could not be revealed. But as I said, events are not always what they seem, you will know soon!*

*Another detail concerning everything that I have just listed for you, because I did not tell you everything, there was also a big family secret. An event that happened exactly on the evening of May 16, 1984, a little before*

*François' grandson told his story, and besides, what was that story?*

*Apart from everything I have told you so far, I put you in context, something prompted Pierre's grandson to speak.*

*One evening, he was with his wife having dinner, the TV on "Antenne 2" (France 2 nowadays). It was raining heavily that night, and lightning made the light bulbs in the dining room sparkle.*

*That same evening, someone knocked on the door, shouting:*

*"Open me please!" There is someone ? "*

*Myriam asked her husband to go see who it was, and with these words the man got up.*

*He came up to the front door and asked:*

*" Who is here ? "*

*and behind the door he answered him!*

*"Open me please, I have something very important to say to you!" "*

*With these words, the man did so and opened the door. An icy wind was blowing through the rooms of the house, and in the background, Myriam, his wife asked to close the door.*

*Her husband says to the stranger:*

*" Go for it ! come in! You will catch death, especially in this outfit! "*

*the stranger returned to the house, looking completely lost, he was shocked, as if he had just had a trauma, and he was agitated on the spot. He told the man who he was, where he came from, while the rain was dripping on the floor.*

*" my God ! "Exclaimed the man" let me bring you something to dry you and dress you warmer, and you will tell me everything once you are dried! And also, calm down! "*

*on these words, the man shouted to his wife*

*"Myriam ! We have a guest! Add a cover! "*

*he went to get a towel and some warm clothes, although a little big, but it was enough for the shivering stranger to warm up a bit!*

*Then this stranger joined the table of his guests, enjoyed a good meal, and exclaimed:*

*"I have never eaten something so good! "*

*and Myriam's husband replied:*

*"You can congratulate my wife, she did it! But back to you! what brings you here at such a late hour? "*

*Tasting a succulent meal, he said the following:*

*"You will take me for a fool if I tell you my story! The simplest is that I show it to you!"*

*"Show us what?" Retorted Myriam's husband.*

*With these words, he asked if he could get out of the table because he had something to collect in his things, he went to the bathroom, and in his jacket pocket, there was a book which he took with him in the dining room join this couple.*

*"A book? Asked the husband "And what is special about this book?""*

*on these words, the guest opened it on the legal notice page where it was noted:*

*Décember \*\*19 – rights reserved*

*It was about the man of the year 1919, but the characters were erased by the rain and replied:*

*"Never heard of this book!" the lead of life? But what is it, then ? "*

*and the stranger replied*

*"This is the year 2019, not the year 1919"*

*"Is that a joke? "Questioned the man*

*"A book written in 2019? Impossible ! "*

*"I assure you that it does!" Read it ! Replied the stranger.*

*Myriam's husband did so, and leafing through the book, although pages were stuck in the rain, he saw his own conversation with this stranger. It seemed to echo with himself, while he was only on page 61, he closed the book, without trying to find out what was next, because he was shocked by what that he had read.*

*But you, reader friends, you may know the story ... ... since this is one of you. You are living it right now and somewhere, in these lines, a new character appears. This book adapts, it evolves and the story can still change, it seems to have no end.*

*And when I say that it has real power, Ho yes! You can take my word for it.*

*I'm going to tell you a fabulous story, one that led me to a spiritual awakening, that let me glimpse a new world. Follow me through the stages of this surreal adventure and let yourself be drawn into an incredible world, the one that concerns me... ..which concerns you.*

If you feel lost in these lines, rest assured, it's normal, because it is part of a huge puzzle that will take shape as you go forward, and also, the author is not fell on your head if that's what you tell yourself!

But strangely enough, the human mind is a bit like this book, with a multitude of overlapping thoughts, but struggling to find a form of coherence. and as surprising as it may seem, this is a good personal development, and I studied the situation well before writing it.

What I'm going to talk to you about are different case figures, retracing all the subtleties of the human mind, because it is a being that is both simple and complex, that has expectations but does not admit it not himself.

The human being has expectations which are not very clear, and to give you an example, concerning those wanting to apply the law of attraction, he has expectations which are in total contradiction, that lacks coherence between what he says and what he thinks, and sometimes between what he thinks and ...... what he thinks (you follow?).

His mind doesn't know exactly what he wants, one day he wants to win the Lotto, the other day he wants to win a very large sum by another means. (which is not quite the same).

For this, I ask you to be very specific about what you ask of the universe, what are your objectives clearly? what do you want to do in life? Imagine that one of your friends asks you to help him build a cabin, and the next day, once a few planks are laid, he asks you to build a bridge, you would say "but what is that you really want? "

Make a road map of what you really want, and stick with it! and the universe will meet your expectations only if that's what you really want.

If, for example, you don't like your job, do you want to find a way to have very good financial security to stop your activity (or even create your own), or do you want to develop your work?

Do you want to win the Lotto, or win a very large sum of money?

As this book which, you will see, is coherent, you too are in the same perspective. Clearly, stay the course towards your projects without deviating from it, and be as stubborn as a Breton, you will see, with consistency, everything will come to you, with, I do not hide perseverance.

## *The gate*

*I ended up buying the book from Myriam, and I don't paid a high price, but the reward that would follow was great, I was far from the 10 € I had to pay, but it was not it was not money. I was entrained in another world, as soon as I started reading the part entitled "The gate".*

*It is from this precise moment, word for word, that everything changed for me, it is here that I left my reality for another one filled with adventures, a real path to unreal, spiritual, and I don't know if it was I who chose this reality, or if it is this "living" book.*

*When I got home, tired of my day, I decided to watch the TV , but there was nothing interesting at this time, it was 8:16 pm, only news with demonstrations in Paris, firefighters who attacked the police. I told myself that the country was going very badly with the demonstrations of yellow vests in* the capital, which took place a few months earlier, and we heard them less and less.

My plate finished, I took the book and looked at it. I was sitting on my chair and looked carefully at the cover of it. There were time-worn prints that I had to force on the view to see them, and I imagined it when it came out, very beautiful, attractive, and there was also this little magic side, and I didn't know why I thought that ..

But after my day chatting about things and things with the merchants in the pits, and wandering the streets, my legs were no longer able to stand on their own and I had a migraine.

I landed on my couch, the book on my stomach, and then started a long nap ... so long that I didn't even know if I was dreaming or if everything I was going to live was real.

*It was like a funny awakening, and I was in a field that seemed outraged by time. what was i doing here? My head was spinning and everything I saw around me was both new and familiar, or at least everything suggested that, where have I seen this place before? there were fields as far as the eye could see, and in the distance there were houses which gave me the impression of deja-vu.*

*Birds were singing melodiously, it was a quiet place and I felt soothed.*

*Not wanting to stay put, I walked towards the houses, there were horses and cows, and a little further, I saw a chicken coop.*

*I approached one of them, the power of this house was attractive, as if an invisible force pushing me right in front of this front door and I rang, and hoping that someone opened me, I saw some familiar thing, a car was parked behind this house, I could only make out the front but it was a Renault Clio of a recent model, maybe from 2010, but in any case, it indicated to me that someone lived here;*

*I heard heels knocking against the tiles, and shortly after there was the sound of a key in the lock. The door opened, and I saw a young woman who looked at me oddly. She asked me:*

*"Hello, how can I help you?" "*

*so, I replied, a little lost that I wanted to know where I was.*

*She replied:*

*"Have you lost your way?" "*

*Unsure of what to say, and remembering why it seemed so familiar to me, this book I had read had given me clues, I asked her the following question:*

*"Am I really on the Dumont farm?"*

*S "Yes, that's how people in the village have called it for a long time! What do I owe the honor of your visit for?"*

*So I told her what I knew, which came from the book I bought a while ago. And also, what convinced her was the story I knew about this stranger who broke into her home, but having stayed long on the landing to give her my story, she made me come into the house . She introduced herself as the owner of the place, her name was Sylvie.*

*Before a cup of coffee, we started a discussion about all that had happened, that during a period of history, this house was on land conquered by the Germans for miles around. She had plenty of time to know her story.*

*S "You know, I had this house for a bite of bread, and the woman who sold it had become a widow and could not manage to get by. I was really sorry for her!"*

*I know what you are saying to yourself at this moment, there is consistency in my story, but wait until you see the rest, because it is quite disturbing.*

*Speaking to the young woman, I said to her:*

*Y "Myriam, is that right?"*

*S "How do you know Myriam?"*

*Y "She was the one who sold me a strange book called 'Viatorem'"*

*Suddenly, the young woman became pensive:*

*S "Viatorem ... ... Viatorem ... ... why do I know this word?"*

*she froze for a moment and told me about this funny fellow who had returned home vomiting*

*S "This guy scared me and my family! He had incoherent remarks, speaking to us about "Viatorem", about epilogue, about the lead of life...... ... he is to this day interned in a psychiatric hospital! "*

*I was asking :*

*"Would it be possible to see it? "*

*and she replied:*

*S "You know? If you are not part of the family, they will not let you in to see him, and unfortunately the poor man has no known family, and they hope that he will one day regain his lucidity and say one day who he is so that he returns to his family who must be worried. "*

*But what I knew about him was that he was part of a story that apparently leaves no hope of returning home to his time, because having not read it herself, she supposed that it was just coincidence, and that after all, it's just a story in a book.*

*At these words, my head started to spin, as if I was still suffering from this bad migraine. What was going on at this precise moment?*

*Pointing out that I was not feeling well and that I was becoming very pale, she said that I could lie on the sofa for a few minutes before leaving if I wanted to.*

*It's uncommon for someone to offer this to a stranger, and taking leave of the conversation and saying I didn't want to disturb her, she said no, and that it was history.*

*I asked him "sorry?" What a story".*

*She replied: "We are all part of a story, and that what I was experiencing was a vision of a reality which is not mine, we are only characters in a book!"*

*Y "But what's going on? Why do you say that?"*

*S "Because we do not exist! Nothing ever existed! In the meantime, I'll get you a Doliprane. Rest for a moment, I feel you need it!"*

*With these words and intrigued, she went to another room. The light was dimming, and everything seemed dark to me, as if night had just fallen, and all of a sudden I heard the woman say something that seemed distant to me, a word like "wuiugup", and I answered "Sorry?*

*She replied "weekub", then, I understood "week-end!"*

*The voice was like far away, but getting louder and louder, I felt like I was being pushed on the arm, and all of a sudden, that voice sounded like another world:*

*"Hey! Yoann, wake up, wake up! WAKE UP !"*

*Then, very slowly, I opened my eyes, and that voice became clearer. My wife was looking me straight in the eyes, I was still lying down, and everything was dark around me. A gleam coming from the TV still on on RMC DECOUVERTE and whose sound was muted, and which gave way to the soft ticking of the pendulum.*

*"What happened? I asked Sophie.*

*S "You fell asleep all dressed on the couch, I worried that I wouldn't see you lying in the bedroom!"*

*On the table, I saw my cat licking the bottom of my plate still placed on the living room table, everything was calm, and I sat on the sofa watching TV without the sound, so I put it back to listen what it was about.*

*It was a program called "La France des mystères" which spoke of a supernatural discovery in Verdun. Construction workers had discovered the bodies of German soldiers buried in the ground. The program said that an excavator had picked up human bones while digging in a construction site for a shopping center.*

*They brought in experts from Germany to identify them, and they had reconciled with documents of the time. But many bodies could not be identified, the only thing known, they were all part of a mystery that has never been solved, because we do not yet know the circumstances of their disappearance, and why they find these bodies only now .*

*it was the mystery of "the ghost division", a sinister name given to this group of men who disappeared during the First World War.*

*But there is a link with this book. Everything finds its coherence in this series of events which are becoming more and more precise. This story is taking shape!*

Is it better to live alone without contact with others? Everyone will tell you, and you probably know it, impossible, because this is what allows us to express who we are, but on the condition of not finding an identity with them, but to seek our own identity . What I mean by that is that it is important to be yourself and no matter where we are and with whom we interact, what is important is to be authentic, without seeking to be a true copy of both the world around us and those who inhabit it.

What man needs is this ability to claim to "be", and also, in a more subtle way, is to adapt to our universe while remaining yourself. This means that you should not express loud and clear this difference which will lead you to a confrontation block against block, your deep nature which you choose to follow, against society and its faults which do not suit you!

As I have already mentioned, in this book as in others, the world is like what you are inside, it is like the two poles of a magnet where opposites repel each other , and the like attract.

We can follow the movement, without rushing, without shocking by living according to our codes, its eccentricities, its creativity.

In this part, we have the example of Pierre, who claims loud and clear to come from the past, but he would have done better to adapt to his environment, because the outside world (his new world), does not accept what 'it claims to be. You have to see the world differently and not try to transform it, let it come to you and don't go looking for it! And if you adapt to this reality by seeing it differently, this difference will come by itself, and you will become what you want!

## *The ghost division*

*In the morning of June 23, 2016 in Verdun, workers take up their position on the site of a project for the construction of a shopping center.*

*one of them finished his coffee, after a discussion with his chef about which side he should dig with his backhoe. The terrain was rugged and swampy, there were many slopes and hollows, outraged by the weather which brought its share of violence and deaths, and the workers knew this very well.*

*We could hear from far away the noise of the backhoe engines and the beep.... Beep.... backwards, the compressors, there were hands waving to indicate directions, and some were screaming to be heard through all the ambient noise.*

*Suddenly someone shouted at the workers:*

*"STOP EVERYTHING! STOP EVERYTHING!"*

*One of the site managers asked all the workers to stop working at the same time.*

*In a bucket, a backhoe had extracted human bones, and they feared they had discovered a crime scene.*

*Numerous phone calls were made to the authorities in the early afternoon, the forensic police asked those still present to leave the area and not to touch anything. The area was secured and marked.*

*In total, the equivalent of 36 bodies were unearthed, but only experts will be able to determine this figure, being based only on the number of skulls found, and personal effects, such as helmets, rifles or pieces of uniform. were able to help determine the origin of the bodies, at least, they knew where they should direct their research.*

*Experts from Germany were dispatched to identify these bodies, using period documents, and an examination room was assigned to them. It was very long to reconstruct each skeleton, and even more to give them a name.*

*There were indeed 36 bodies, and some skeletons lacked elements, a femur, a forearm, ribs ...... and only 21 were able to recover their identity, thanks to the identification plates, the remains could be returned to descendants.*

*The mystery remained complete as to the 15 bodies remaining, as there was absolutely nothing to identify them.*

*The field became a zone of archaeological excavations, scientists were present with their small brushes to delicately remove each grain of dust, and sifted through everything they found, and there were inconsistencies as to the place of discovery.*

*Indeed, they also discovered elements dating back to the Napoleonic era, rusty sabers, remains of what could have been a belt, and a plaque with an imperial eagle. And the conclusion they had was that there had been events on this same ground, at two separate and unrelated eras, for them it was just a combination of circumstances, at least in appearance.*

*But when samples were taken from these discoveries, they wanted to date them to carbon 14, and they were astonished, because these two seemingly unrelated events were part of the same space ...... .but also of a same time, and it was determined that all that had been discovered had the same seniority, around 1800.. ..*

*Something a little disturbing too, was the remnants of what looked like a metal case that seemed familiar to these researchers, an oxidized rectange. Further analysis revealed something. After cleaning and analyzing the spectrum, an inscription was discovered, barely noticeable, like engraved letters, and what was readable was just an A and NG at the end.*

*One of them said "SAMSUNG?"*

*Impossible, shouted one of the experts, there must have been an error, or the samples were contaminated.*

*Some time later, a team of journalists having heard of this discovery was dispatched to the scene. Authorities spoke of the 21 bodies unearthed in a grave, only 21 of which had been kept under wraps for a few months before one of the scientists exposed the matter in the open on a video posted on YouTube. His face was masked and his voice altered to conceal his identity.*

*Speculation? Conspiracy theories? Information circulated on the web, and comments were rife, sometimes in childish settling of scores between commentators to demonstrate who was more right than the other.*

*However, the story does not end there! Because, this revelation was not passed over in silence, even for the authorities who did everything to find this scientist who had sold the wick. They didn't have too much trouble finding the person.*

*RMC DECOUVERTE returned to these surreal events, those I saw on my TV screen, as if captivated by this story. It was 4:27 a.m. and I hadn't gone to bed yet. I became like an insomniac, absorbed as part of this story.*

*Strangely, soon after the program and looking at my book, I discovered it at my expense. I was looking at it on the last page I had read and I wanted to know a little more about my meeting with Sylvie.*

*There was a form of continuity in reading the continuation, and I remembered what Sylvie had told me, that we are all part of a story, and this was confirmed in the pages of "Viatorem".*

*Funny coincidence, because he also spoke about this word for word, and I was drawn in spite of myself into a funny story that spoke of this ghost division ... ... and of me. what was i doing in it?*

*As I said, and I learned it as I read, it's that this book decides everything, we have no control over it, it's he who owns us!*

*After reading a few passages, I went to rest. It was around 7:30 am and it's one of the few times I go to bed early in the morning.*

## *1802*

*I was sleeping in a deep sleep when a cold wind invaded my face. There were like drops of water touching my skin, and they seemed to go on forever. Like starry masses without brilliance but icy, the feeling that I was no longer, but that I remained in other places as strange as familiar.*

*My eyelids finally opened and I discovered all around me a magical whiteness accompanied by a sky like blood, a winter magic which only made illusion with the context in which it was.*

*Death reigned supreme, he had sent his mower over this field, or the words gave way to screams, you could barely make out groans of youthful pain that seemed to be muffled by the sound of cannons.*

*Sudden fear took hold of me, but where did I land? It was hell ? If so, the devil wears a weapon!*

*I was there in this environment, my clothes soaked, I felt like I had come out of the shower with the water heater turned off.*

*The smell of rotting flesh had nothing to do with the smell of dead animals, I took a few steps in this snowy coat, and something seemed to grab my ankle. It was a hand ..... a hand hidden beneath this cold, whitish layer.*

*I had never seen a dead human, and I was not very excited to see one, and that hand let me know what else was going on.*

*in the distance, I live like motionless shadows, like petrified like statues of ice, they were soldiers, and under the snow, I had not recognized the uniforms, They seemed French, and dated from a long time ago or the desire for conquest was stronger than the love of one's neighbor, for there is no heart that would resist a dagger.*

*This beautiful promise made by an emperor whose enthusiastic tone was mixed with unconsciousness, but what a bitter taste these poor cold men had if they had known what they would endure.*

*Although strange, this cold place, whose history I knew, reminded me of another, in the form of a machine gun noise.*

*"How was it possible?" ", There was this phantom division that came back to my mind, these men lost out of time, we seemed brothers in such circumstances, we were time travelers, but so many things separated us, generation and culture differentiated us .*

*These, of which I did not understand a word traitor of the Germanic language, seemed to make signs in my direction, whereas one did not know each other, and there was this strange word, so close ..... ..Viatorem ....*

*They shouted that word at me, but were they really looking at me?*

*"Viatorem ....... Viatorem ......" they said frightened, but I quickly realized that it was only an illusion, and that their eyes wet by the flakes did not look at me, but something else that goes beyond the lines of this book, they felt like they saw an invisible being beyond this simple passage, as if to pierce the sky.*

*I turned around, and I saw him, this being who had his eyes riveted as if to read a book, and it was you, unconscious and surprised, yes, you! This reality does not exist, you are just a story in a book, held by New Prussians, but what did you do to make them so afraid?*

*So distracted by your intervention, they did not pay attention to the massive arrival of the fifteen men brandishing a weapon, they did not even have time to reload their machine gun that they had to face and fight to equal arms, fists and steel.*

*All this time, I stayed in the same place, to observe, I was soaked, but the cold did not make me shiver, the scene I witnessed was a meeting with my first experience of death, it was like a trauma, frozen and frightened .*

*When the assault was over, I got closer, but not very excited to see corpses. I stumbled upon one of them finding myself on the ground face to face with cold pulpit and a blank stare.*

*I passed out, and I heard myself as a cavalry which was going to launch the assault, and it was at this precise moment that I woke up, always with this impression which mixes real and imaginary. With the TV always on on a documentary retracing the epic of the French cavalry, the images were in black and white, as if taken from an old film from the 1950s.*

Man has always been a fighter, but not in the warlike sense of the word. He always wanted to control the elements, but it is the elements that control him, and he dreams with his eyes open.

Fighting against the elements is a futile objective if it goes into speculative and defeatist drifts, because it programs itself for self sabotage.

The only way out is by forgetting what being is, to make room for new thoughts, outside the outside world, because he is his own creator, and he can do anything with will. It means acting without worrying about what the outside world (those around you and the acquaintances) told him to be devastating to feel the urge to take action, moreover, I will come back to this soon.

The human did not lose the desire to fight, because he never had it, because he learned that it was too hard, that he was incapable of it from an early age, c is the nerve center of all that being is meant to be.

That it is useless to fight without a battle plan against a better prepared adversary, and that he is oblivious to want to attack on all fronts, which does not really clear up a single precise goal, fragmented into others which its hit and miss.

We can win a battle, but not the war, and also we can lose one, which also does not mean the imminent defeat of the conflict.

Only clear objectives make us advance, and that it is more courageous the one who advances on the steps that he himself has traced, than in the wake of others, or by creating them in a moving ground.

Always act in the clearest and fairest way for you, without listening to the mistaken apprioris of the universe around you, without chasing time, take it to focus on what you are doing towards the goal, and not focus on the goal.

## *The encounter*

*It was after 2:15 p.m. when I woke up, and I was alone in my apartment, well almost, there was my cat still sleeping, and I tell myself that he is very lucky to be able to rest, the looking serene and happy, turning and almost taking acrobatic postures.*

*Everything was quiet, just the ticking of the pendulum and a few horns outside. It's not easy to live in the city center, in all this hustle and bustle, from the top of my benchmark, I can observe like thousands of ants that run all the time without knowing where to go, and without worrying about knowing that a whole other universe is possible.*

*Preparing to go out to face this crowd, and make my way to my next destination, I barely put on my jacket when the doorbell rang.*

*"Who's there?" I asked this person behind the front door.*

*"Please open!", It is important "replied a voice which resounded in the hall," I need to speak to you "*

*„And who are you?"*

*"A friend you know very well!"*

*before this insistence, and going out in any case, I opened the door which separated me from this stranger, and found me facing him.*

*Y "I'm listening to you! What can I do for you? I still have a few minutes, then I have to go find my partner "*

*A "For that, don't worry! You have all your time, I explain everything you want to know about the book you have!"*

*"How do you know this book?"*

A *"I don't know if you're going to believe me, but imagine that I know the person who wrote it, then can I sit down for a few minutes to explain all this to you?"*

Y *"I don't understand a word about what you want with me, and you pretend to know the person who wrote this book?"*

To *"she is much closer than you can imagine! You know? I know you very well, even by heart!"*

*"Is this me the author who wrote this book? Does it come from my future self? That would explain why the author bears my name!"*

A *"Oh no great god! don't even think about it! And what idea to write a book that already exists? I've been watching you Yoann for a while, and you surprise me on every page of this book!"*

Y "What do you mean? You know what happened before in the pages of this book? And how come he talks about me?"

A "Simply because you are only a character that I created and all that you live is my universe, it comes from my inspiration"

Not knowing where he got this information, and not finding it very clear, because something in him did not inspire confidence in me, I replied:

Y "I don't know who you are and you pretend to be a friend of mine, it doesn't make me laugh at all! I would ask you to get out of here, you made me waste enough time like that!"

turning towards the door, this stranger said to me the following thing:

To "Too bad Yoann! Too bad! ...... Too bad! Pity! Too bad!... .. (sighing), I don't know *what Sophie, who is currently at her mother's house, and who is having tea… ..or coffee… would think, will notify!"*

*What are you telling me? And how do you know about…."*

*he interrupts me*

*"Her mother lives at 38 rue des Mimosas in Verdun, her name is …… (snaps of her fingers) …… Suzanne, am I wrong? I'd be surprised! And you don't need to take your cell phone anyway, it stayed in 1802!"*

*Indeed, after searching my pockets and looking everywhere, he was nowhere to be found … .. Would I have lost him when I tripped over one of the soldiers?*

*Y and A at the same time:*
*"And how … … did … .."*

*A "I anticipate everything you are going to say or do, and there is no point in challenging me, you only exist because I really want it!"*

*Y "why do you say this? And where do you get all this information from?"*

*A "Because I decided it! All this information, I just wrote it on this page, and since you insisted on knowing who I am, I am the author of this book, a book of which you are the main character, check it for yourself - even on page 102, we are still having this conversation."*

*All of a sudden, my whole universe collapsed! He knew a lot of information about me and my entourage*

*"Does that mean I don't exist?""*

*To "My dear friend, you are just the product of my fertile imagination, and this so-called real life that you believe to live so much, it does not exist! You are nothing more than a fictional character, even if everything seems real to you. And it is at this insistence to believe that you are real that I must intervene! What you'll find inside this book will exceed all your expectations."*

*"What expectations are you talking to me about?"*

*A "Knowing the truth, and this is what surprised me most about you! You seemed so human, so present, that I was afraid that you would take control of my work! I was afraid that you would endocrine all the characters here in these pages, and that you would rewrite history in your own way! Nothing belongs to you here! You are at home, and this is my world!"*

*Still reeling from what I had just learned! My head was spinning and I couldn't balance on my two legs anymore.*

*A "You are very pale my dear friend, sit down for a moment and do not worry in any way about Sophie, she can wait as long as I decide! Contrary to what you may think, I am not your enemy, and if I intended to harm you, I would have done it a long time ago, and I don't need much for that! And it may even be that ..... "*

*(He paused for a moment!)*

*A "I can't answer you! We are being watched!"*

*Y "Who are you talking about?"*

*A "From the one who is reading this book!""*

*Looking in the same direction as the author, I saw that you were on page 104, watching us.*

*Y "Hello to you traveler, if I can call you that! are you all right? I know! this story seems very strange to you, but don't worry, it will take on its full meaning when you join us ...... soon ...... very soon ......! "*

*A "We are waiting for you!" It shouldn't be very long anymore, your place is ready for our adventures! "*

*Y "Perhaps we should discuss all this among ourselves, in secret from the reader! "*

*A "It would be better indeed, and what I have to say to you only concerns you Yoann! "*

*On this interview, we discussed a little while and the author explained to me what he expected from me.*

*He explained to me that his book had gotten out of control and that the story he had written had taken a different turn. He told me about this strange world, halfway between real and imaginary. And he also said that the guardian of the temple was responsible for this disorder. But who was this guardian?*

*Maybe you too, reader friends, are in a book and think you are alive. Only, our human nature makes us believe everything we want to believe or hope, but hope is only the assumption of a tomorrow, one that may never come, and in basically, what do you really decide in the world you live in?*

There are always bigger than us! An author decides who we are, and what we think we are. And when you understand how your lives are controlled, it is possible that you will revise your judgments, and that you are only a modest appearing in a dramatic comedy.

As I said, there is always more powerful than us, but we can control it, you will understand more fully this amalgam which stuns your consciousness still dormant, but I learned ... ... learned to reach this state of full awareness and that it is possible to be the conductor of our existence thanks to our inner power, the one who dominates it, it is our creative genius, which allows us to advance very far, to cross kilometers without to be breathless.

Man has been deprived of all of his ability to act for himself, because he has not attempted to see his universe larger. He is just a character who has a scenario, and no matter which direction he goes, if he has not taken the initiative to see otherwise, that is, without relying on his mental formatting, he will get tirelessly the same results.

if there were to choose, I would ask you, reader friends, to be in the camp of the winners, and this is where your place should remain, because I will tell you words which most of them do not have felt all the power:

"I believe in you and you are capable of much more than you can imagine!"

only, it remains only to convince you!

The master teaches, and the student must become the master, that is, if he learns to become responsible, he must apply all his knowledge to lead the next generation to this control of existence.

All that the human being needs is this power that he has to control his actions, to make decisions, and he learns it to his depend one day when the forces of nature forces him to become better autonomous, independent, without waiting for something from his elders. Everything is already in him, the power of responsibility, of decision, of thoughtful initiatives, and he is really the only actor to take charge of his life. It is to be a leader and not a follower. Expect more from yourself.

What I have learned this life is that it is important to hold on to your dreams and dominate them without being dominated by them. No one has power over it, just empty words whether or not you listen to them.

Everything is gradually being put together, reader friends, the whole story, you have it in front of you, but it does not end there. Because you only explored a fragment of this magic book.

My adventure was just beginning, and in the lines of this book, it is about a quest between the imaginary and the real, and if you believe that this book has no meaning, it has one, but you don't see it yet, or maybe you can see its outline.

Here is the story that the author chose for me, he has planned a scenario that will make you travel in a strange world, filled with characters as curious as each other. It is about a quest towards the guardian of the temple, I did not know what that meant, but just like me, you will understand! it is a journey with stages, each of which has deep meaning.

You are part of this story and you live it every day, this is how it started .......

# Act II
# The temple

*In this place of a thousand secrets*

*The guard is at the entrance*

*One piece in hand*

*Resounded in the distance*

## Step 1:
## The Guardian

*"As long as we work, produce, think, act, shine, we give ourselves the illusion of being, we defend ourselves against desolation and despair. If the city is in ash, we take refuge in the citadel; if the citadel is taken one withdraws in the central reduction. "*
*(Henri-Frédéric Amiel; Diary, June 10, 1877)*

*I was born the day I opened my eyes, but it was not in 1978, but more recently in a burst, during a night when I couldn't sleep anymore, overwhelmed by my problems, I discovered the spiritual awakening.*

*This place seemed unfamiliar to me until that moment when the real world opened up to me, and my whole life was only an illusion, formatted in a world that followed what I would call "conventions".*

*This great revelation is that we are beings formatted by a system and we have unconsciously signed a pact with it, preventing me from seeing beyond my imagination, extricating myself from my refuge, from my dreams.*

*What did this individual who called himself the author want with me? I don't know yet, but he took me on an adventure in search of the deeper self. He wanted me to discover a world of which I was not aware.*

*I do not remember how I crossed this border between the imaginary and the real, and I was in search of the guardian of the temple, I did not know if my trip would be long, but I set off towards a goal which seemed inaccessible to me.*

*But where was I really? In the fertile imagination of an author, or was it just a bad dream? It was this famous morning in June 2019, and I came out of my daze, lost in my thoughts, but the fact remains that a jolt made me regain consciousness. It was Sophie, she was in front of me waving her hands and telling me*

*S "Hého! Yoann! Are you still with me?" (Snapping my fingers)*

*I shook myself like an animal that snorts, and what I finally saw was, in my opinion, reality ...... This is what I was hoping for ....*

*We were on the bridge just opposite the palace of L'isle in Annecy, and my partner looked at me oddly as if she was looking at a curious beast.*

*S "Where have you been?"*

*Y "What do you mean?""*

*What is that? You haven't answered me for 5 minutes, you were disconnected from me, are you sure you're okay?"*

Y *"Er ..... yes yes! Alright sweetie! I don't know why I was elsewhere in my thoughts!"*

S *"Hey bein! I don't know what you did last night, but you seem asleep! Come on! We are going now! We have to find a restaurant, and I hope you will be with me to eat ...... face to face, if it's still possible for you!"*

*On these words, and still pensive, I wondered how it was possible to have had the impression of living a lifetime. But my partner had already lost patience, and we had to move on.*

*We stopped to eat "Au Munich" where we ordered fried dishes accompanied by fries. The setting was ideal by the canal, there were swans with their cubs swimming under the gaze of tourists who did not hesitate to take photos of this small family.*

*Shortly after our lunch, we wandered along the canal to the sound of a violin that a street artist was using. Under a cheerful air, the music seemed out of context, because despite this enchantment of Peynet lovers, at every corner of this big city (like all big cities), we could not escape this vision of ambient misery, and I was hardly for them.*

*Where had that magic gone that was in them when they were younger? The disillusionment seems to have taken over, leaving no room for dreams, and their whole universe had collapsed, faced with this sad reality.*

*One of them looked at me, and I didn't know how to help him other than by giving a coin. But how long would this give balm to this misery?*

*But he spoke to me, and on the other hand, my partner pulled my arm*

*S "Come on! Come ! Let's go ! " (angry)*

*But what he said to me briefly, taken from another side, as if it was going to rip my arm, reminded me of my dreams of not long ago.*

*The beggar:*
*"Remember that reality is not what it seems! Get out of this book! Look for the temple guardian!"*

*But I don't know any more! Sophie hurried on and her heels clicked on the pavement towards our car.*

We learn to think more with our heads than with our hearts, bombarded with false beliefs from a watered-down society that made me a so-called accomplished being, grown up, powerful, but limited in movement.

My universe was comparable to that of a fish in a bowl or a bird in its cage, and I dominated this universe. But the universe is larger than that, it is not limited to the top of a perch or the top of the jar, and I thought I was invincible, superior, but outside of this spiritual state.

All these years of believing that I could not reach a state superior to that in which I was plunged, indoctrinated by sentences such as "you will not succeed! ", " your are so null ! "," The world is like this! Or "this is life! But also, did those who declared these sentences find a solution to their situation? Have they resigned themselves to no longer advancing?

I'm taking you on a wonderful journey, beyond your compartmentalized imagination, beyond what you can see or hear, this state that seems irrational, what you call "madness", I call this "the state of mindfulness ".

What you think you know will no longer exist, unless your subconscious tells you otherwise. Learn to open your mind more and you will understand that you are not where you should be, but elsewhere, thanks to the imagination and the extension of its possibilities.

You can continue to live your life quietly, following the conventions, a small tidy life, a woman and children, a job that you do not like very much, but you make with, and a meager salary preventing you from making ends of months or have hobbies.

But there is another possibility, that of signing new agreements with yourself, thus revealing your true nature, a new pact. It's a world that may seem strange to you at first glance, but will challenge everything you've learned so far.

You are intelligent beings, capable of great prowess, a state that exceeds fear and doubt, but perhaps you do not know it yet, or you think you know it.

There is no limit to the imagination, except those that you give yourself or that you have been entrusted with, and you must also be daring and crazy, opening up your artistic and creative side, what I am currently doing with this book.

There is an eccentric side which only asks to wake up, that in connection with your deep being which is hidden in your heart, it is your soul which knows what is good for you or not, and currently, you feel uncomfortable, unhappy, because you seem to be in conflict with yourself, your burning desires burning in you, why?

Because you simply put more trust in what you were told, what you learned, using your head and very little your heart, and what you have in your mind is just a bank of data of information which you accepted not in your soul and conscience, a formatting in the community standards believing to make hard with soft.

These standards that we learn in schools, in churches, taught by humans and not by God Himself, telling you what is right or wrong, teaching you to be good citizens, to work, to pay your taxes, and above all, do not revolt.

But this God is in relation to our deep nature, and unconsciously, you have already crossed him more than once so he is intimate with you, and he always advised you, supported you, but you did not hear him, and when you reason better with your heart, you will begin to discern what it dictates to you.

No longer be beings subject to the collective conscience, and come and join the ranks of those who have freed themselves from conventions, they had their independence thanks to their imagination, which is the madness of geniuses.

This little bit of madness that you miss, this fear of being judged simply because you want to be yourself, this conviction that you have to think like the others to be like the others and that, whatever the social status, you don't fully live your existence, and it's sad to see.

Open the doors of your heart, and have a little more extravagance, there are authors, artists, musicians, or philosophers who succeed, because they are in agreement with themselves and are not beings subject to a societal dictate, and who understood very early on that it was necessary to be different, original with a touch of madness.

From then on, you will reach this state of grace, the openness of mind towards an infinite universe. And when you understand this, you save your soul.

It may seem far-fetched what I am telling you there and I understand you, but use your heart to ask yourself the question "who are you really?" "

We all have this magic inside us, the power to create our refuge in an imaginary world where there are no limits, around unusual places filled with fantastic beings, and where you can be whoever you want.

Inside your imagination is a treasure that you can take with you, if you have enough faith. The secret for it to materialize lies in your heart, and when you reach this state of mindfulness, anything will be possible. I am not asking you to believe me, but to believe in yourself!

The adult man has become a being unable to dream, to see beyond his possibilities, because the real world has taken over, and he thinks for himself.

Reveal your extravagant, artistic side, be the artist of your life. I'm taking you on a wonderful journey populated by individuals at every stage of this journey. Dream a little and relax, happiness is present in these pages, and you will discover who is your leader, that of your life.

*No gallows nor judged*

*Rope stretched without condemned*

*The woman is the ringer's shelter*

*Pointing to the creator*

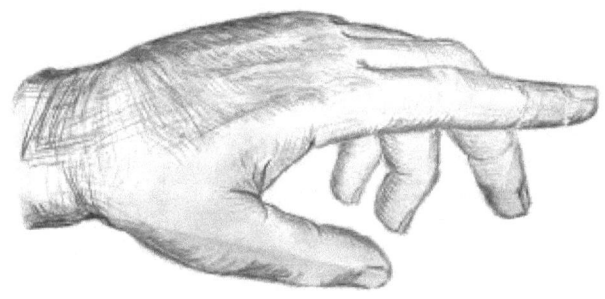

## 2nd step
## The drawer

*May I be given the strength to endure what can be changed and the courage to change what can be but also the wisdom to distinguish one from the other.*
*Marc Aurèle*
*(Emperor, Statesman,*
*Philosopher (121-180))*

We were, me and my wife, on the way to our destination, at the passage of Groisy, La Roche sur Foron, Bonneville, and Vougy, we decided not to stop at our place, and make a detour on Cluses to go for a coffee each.

But we were tired, after walking for a long time in the city of Annecy, we needed this boost, and it was only 9:13 p.m. This allowed me, even if the road was not that long, to relax a bit before getting back into the car.

*The evening went rather well, and after returning to our home, we had seen our cat resting on the sofa. He was so peaceful, like a child you wouldn't dare wake up. Apart from that, everything seemed calm, and I had turned on the TV to put an end to the heavy silence.*

*I sat on the couch making sure not to touch our sleeping friend, and I zapped on shows of little interest to me or my partner, anyway, she was gone in the bathroom. And I stopped on the Discovery Channel.*

*There was this show hosted by Chip Foos titled "Overhaulin". I do not hide one of my passions for car restorations, I also love history and science, with always this desire to discover, appreciate, love life, and I prefer this to the news speaking than violence and roosters. There are men who can do more harm with a feather than with a dagger, but let's go back to our story.*

*So, I was watching the program animated by Chip Foos, this one consists in refurbishing, in a personalized way, legendary cars belonging to owners who are surprised to be selected for a complete restoration of these.*

*And at one point during the broadcast, I saw someone close to the owner of the vehicle telling Chip Foos the preferences he wanted, red body color, small block engine, Shelby style, etc. sides, Chip was drawing the vehicle based on the information gathered.*

*When he had finished drawing, Chip showed the drawing of the dream vehicle ....... well, that's what I thought ..... but something caught my eye.*

*Instead of announcing the owner's name, he said:*

*"Yoann, this message is for you!" "*

*Y "Huh? What? "*

*The message Chip was showing me on the other side of my TV screen said the following!*

*"Look for the lost child!"*

*What did that mean? Wasn't my quest just to find the temple guardian? And besides, was this adventure real? Am I still dreaming? In the hands of an author who manipulates me according to his desires? But where am I? Real or imaginary?*

*My wife was shaking me*

*Wake up Yoann! Are you still sleeping!"*

*Returning to "reality" and opening my eyes very slowly, I saw my wife, with that facial expression that spoke volumes about her state of mind, but yet ...*

*S "Go in search of the lost child Yoann! You have to find it!"*

*Y "What are you telling me darling?"*

*And a few seconds later, my vision was clouded, I fell into a deep sleep, and took me to places that were completely unknown to me.*

We are all artists at heart, because every day we draw our lives, but on what basis do we do it?

Your mind needs to identify with someone or something, and we all do. We have our own heroes, our own icons, and we just look like what we worship, no more and no less.

It has an external context to build on, but without it, what would you be? Without the foundations of education (in the broadest sense of the term), there would be no identity. With no one around and no social status, the mind is just an empty shell.

We all want to look like someone, our father, our mother, a TV or movie star, and we learn to become that. And somewhere, there is a background of frustration when we do not succeed, for example, changing social status to become a star, like our "hero", our "icon".

Clearly, drawing your image around someone does not mean being someone, it is just becoming a pale copy of your idol, and to sum it all up, you no longer have your own existence, but you find your identity with others. And without this support, the human spirit is nothing but an empty shell. You therefore live in a reality in which you do not exist!

Imagine a person alone in the desert, he was born in this hostile climate with no surrounding soul who lives there, so no context on which his mind can rely.

But if it encounters a tree for the first time in its life, the brain begins to create what is called a "neuro-association" relating to pleasure or disgust, good or bad.

We combine things like emptiness and fear, chocolate ice cream and fun. But not everyone associates this in the same way, such as the fulambulist who appreciates the strong sensations of emptiness, or the child who does not like chocolate.

And it is thus an accumulation of this information which creates a system unique to each individual, a way of thinking which is specific to each one, but which he does not own.

This information does not come by itself, it is based on the environment and the social and family context.

Thought becomes icon, and everyone uses the image to exist, and what I call "the icon" is the symbolism of all the information perceived from youth until now, your current life.

Have you wondered why you like or hate chocolate ice cream? Have you ever wondered why you like to be afraid of the void and challenge the elements?

"The icon" is the symbol, bad or not, associated with a past and resounding experience in the present, and that is why, and I suspect myself a little knowing perfectly human nature, that some people find my remarks absurd, and others not, and I reassure you right away, each one being unique, you are right in both cases. Because everyone is unique and not everyone will react the same according to experience.

Basically, who are you really? And who am I personally? I'm an author, an actor, a creator and a viewer of my own life, but I could very well be called by other names according to everyone's beliefs.

What designates me as a whole being is not the fact that I am the author of books (of which this one reaches a whole other dimension).

the being is invisible, intangible and not named, but he lives at the bottom of each of us. Maybe we don't want to see it or hear it, because we are convinced "to be".

But what I'm about to teach you is going to be a game-changer. I am not directly the author of this book!

What I mean by that is that my knowledge belongs to the people who have accompanied me in my life, and that I recognize that I have no identity of its own, it is based on the learning of life. And that sums up very well what I'm going to tell you, that ultimately, we only exist through others, and humans are not made to be alone in all situations of life.

the human mind is built from outside elements, and it's from these that our creativity and emotions work.

What belongs to me is the way it was developed, it is also the thoughts of the soul expressed through words which are not mine, but which belong to my teaching staff when I was younger. .

What is certain for ordinary people is that it is not!

You are free to think from birth but artificially, making you believe in a pseudo freedom to choose the life you want, but you fell into a societal trap, a massive formatting crowned with false convictions, and you learned with your head and not with your heart, and you did not open yourself further, because you were told that it was impossible, null, inaccessible, but your soul expressed itself over and over again, but you did not not listened to, it has manifested itself more than once in the form of dreams, and your very down to earth conception has rejected its requests. So you get up every morning to go to work, to fuel a consumer society, and to pay taxes.

The human being is a free and unconscious being, as free as a canary in a large aviary, it may seem large enough, but it seems impossible to him to go beyond, because one made him believe this stupidity. Unable to dream, imagine, without being taken for a madman, or an original in the best of cases, and the universe has endowed him with an immense power, that of being!

You are not lost my cute, far from it, and when you get to the end of this book, if you have enough courage and the will to really want to dominate the events, your way of thinking will have literally changed, and you will no longer think like the others, but in relation to your deepest aspirations. You will finally be! In the spiritual awakening phase.

What you need above all is to get out of these codes and conventions and to be free to be who you want, to discover your true nature, the one you do not want to know for fear of being ridiculed.

Human beings follow certain protocols related to the mass effect, to be like the popular majority who inflicted blue on you while deep down you like red (will understand who will).

Basically, we are not the people we seem to be, we have been imposed on us with patronymic and moral identities that are not ours, but chosen by those around us, we do not choose our last name and first name any more than validate in our soul and conscience what is right or not!

On your identity card, your name is Pierre, Paul or Jacques, and you exercise a profession, but concretely, who are you or who would you be if you could choose? Be inspired and act according to what your heart dictates.

An artist has demonstrated this in a series of paintings representing fruits or objects. This is René Magritte in his works entitled "The betrayal of images".

Our perception is therefore very limited to the fields of the known by ordinary people, but the symbolism goes far beyond simple images which have defined it very well or badly.

The human enjoys a very great ignorance of the field of the possible, and in another universe, if you had learned that a table was in fact a chair, it goes without saying that in this current universe, you would have been taken for a mad person.

In my opinion, and what René Magritte has demonstrated, whether it be an apple, a pear, a chair, a table, or whatever, whatever name we can give to these objects or fruits, what is most important is the function and not the nominative character.

I teach you that your perception is misleading, and you make a block on the rational linked to certain beliefs.

what you see or feel as impossible is not it possible? why not ? are you afraid of being something other than what you are now, but what you do not yet know is that you have always "been" deep inside, and you will still be.

We quickly get ideas about a given situation, for example, if you meet a person wearing a very nice suit, does that mean that he has money? and if he is in a bank, with a bouquet of flowers and he walks towards the counter, what are you going to assume? is he going to flirt with her, or is he just withdrawing money, and he has to go to a funeral right after? you know what basically?

Let us not be betrayed by what we see! don't have a bad impression of yourself or others!

To think that you are null, incapable, gifted, intelligent, they are only "images", it is the perception which you have, and you represent yourself in relation to that, according to what you have been affirmed, but you are the only one who chooses who you really want to be.

you see successful people, so what?
there are others who fail, so what?

failure and success is all about you, not others who just go their way. and if you have the image of success in you, affirm it, deep down, without waiting or believing the judgments of others. Do not be happy or disappointed with what you see, it is the outside world, and the same goes for "they say that", or "congratulations", or "it sucks". it belongs to the outside world, and no one needs to think for you.

Each human being is his own "victory" or "defeat"! and when you have truly understood the meaning of this statement, you will advance by leaps and bounds in life.

Never trust appearances, they are deceptive, and that I cannot repeat it enough!

I will tell you a little further about a personality who knew how to face an identity wall, but who knew how to get around it by choosing who he was really deep inside, and who shone with his deep aspirations, I will tell you the story of Korla Pendit which will prove to you that the only limits are those that we impose on ourselves.

*It weighs heavier than a feather*

*But only related to the horizon*

*Its story is not clay*

*Oceans and mists*

*Were his condition*

## Step 3:
## The child

*"Every child is in a way a genius, and every genius a child."*
*(Arthur Schopenhauer)*

*I found myself locked in my own mind, and from that moment on, the world that I knew (or thought I knew) no longer existed. The real seemed only an illusion in which I was languishing in uncertainty.*

*I was in what looked like a busy street, but I knew it was only my imagination. It reminded me of strange memories, these streets, these houses and these people were familiar to me, like a scene repeating itself.*

*There were men and women walking around with their children (assuming it was their own), and I noticed that they had two each time, a boy and a girl.*

*A little curious about these provisions, I tried to find a scheme to learn more about them:*

*"Hello Mr. Lady, I need some information, where are we?" "*

*The man answers me:*

*"Yoann, right? "*

*Y "How do you know my first name? "*

*H "It is everywhere on the pages of this book, no wonder we know that, and also, you are in your own thoughts, and it is more precisely your memories! "*

*Taken aback by the fact that he knows the book that has taken me on mysterious adventures, I began to think about my meeting with the author, would I be just a fictional character? And yet everything seemed very real to me. I recognized the environment of my youth, everything had remained the same, at the same time, the scents, the feelings and what I saw, everything seemed in its place, as if frozen in time. It was wonderful, there was still this grocery store where I was going to buy candy right after school. There were even these milk deposits that were put on a cart in exchange for a few coins.*

*But something was wrong, and I didn't know what it was, but the answer came from this lady who was with her partner.*

*D "Where did your child go?" "*

*Y "Sorry? I have no children! Why this question ? "*

*D "Everyone takes with them a child of their own. We all have them here, but I and my partner do not share the same. "*

*She pointed out to me that of all the people present at this place, I was the only one who had no children. But his remark was astonishing. The two people in front of me seemed to tell me they each had a child, but they weren't in common.*

*D "My dear friend, we always take a child with us, he always lives with us and grows with us. He is the same age and reminds us of where we come from. and no matter what situation you go through in life, he is always there, keen and amused in this world."*

*During this interview, I remembered what had happened a little earlier when I was still awake. What my partner and Chip Foos had told me about what to look for. But it could only exist in one place. And I had to follow a path leading straight to him, and had to go through the reunion with old emotions that I thought were extinct, and hide everything I knew about this "real" world.*

*The path I was taking now was chaotic, having to weave between rejection of reality and disillusionment. And what appeared before me seemed very random. No visibility, emptiness, and for only reference, a plan that I had to follow scrupulously.*

*And absorbed by this road map, I heard the cry of a child in the distance. And the more I revived old emotions, the closer the tears were.*

*He was there ! not very far from me, and the road approaching my goal made this little being more visible, and it was now a stone's throw from me that I asked him this question:*

*"What are you doing here young boy, and why are you crying?" "*

*the child drying his tears on his sleeves answered me:*

*"I cry because I am lost"*

*He hastened to ask him why he was lost and replied:*

*"Because adults can no longer dream!" "*

*So, very surprised at his answer, I asked him why they could no longer dream.*

*Listening attentively, I understood that this child was me younger.*

*He told me that he was in the company of his creative genius, but that the man he calls "the judge" had kidnapped him. Leaving the child alone in an empty environment, having nowhere to go and not knowing where it was. His only guide was what the judge had told him, and that there was no other way to go.*

*Then he told me the following:*

*"If you find my creative genius, I will help you find the way to the guardian of the*

*temple. He is the one who knows all the routes leading to him."*

*I promised to go and confront the judge and unleash his creative genius, on this interview, I resumed my journey.*

Growing up, we lose sight of everything that motivated us, and our world that we created for ourselves fell into absurdity in the face of a very harsh environment, filled with people judging our capacities to create new things.

Childhood is the future of humanity, it is it, through its imagination that puts colors in the gray of our lives, it is precious and we are, in some ways the protectors of this youth with a fertile spirit.

We keep traces of this child that we were, full of creativity, seeing the world differently, slender and full of future, and his companion, the creative genius, is still there, locked in a pandora's box by those who have shattered our dreams, in order to follow the established order like wise little robots, showing us that it is impossible to be other than what we are.

These beliefs have taken firm hold in us from year to year, and that is why, dear readers, that most of you do not understand everything I am telling you, because your world has become something. absurd, impossible to achieve, and you no longer reason with the heart of a child, because you tell yourself that once an adult, it's no longer worth it.

But the child deep inside is just asking to speak, let him help you find your creative genius!

What has lost humanity is that it listened to the outside world too much, overwhelmed by false images that cheated with our deep convictions of "being", but in the end, who are we really? What did our family tell us? Our friends ? Our colleagues? The media? Unconsciously, we have become in the image of the outside world, and all that can harm human beings is to live with this pseudo feeling of being free to choose, but to choose what precisely?

Yes, since childhood, and it was a dirty habit, the human has become a character dependent on the image we gave him, as well as the world around him, and that's what he happens in teaching, it provides images that are not its own, or at least, those wanted if it had the capacity.

We live through limiting beliefs, but which are not representative of the real world, because this is what we make of it without free will, one more thing that does not exist! We have this ability to imagine the world in our own way, not conceptual, not generated by a sneaky dictate, as if hypnotized in a dummy bubble of well-being. But real freedom is to accept to continue to believe that we are outside this system or not, to want to see differently or not.

There is no situation in the world capable of helping the child to believe in himself and his dreams, to listen to him or to follow his expectations, because the child is never heard. We just lay the foundations for an unfair and perverted world, teaching him that he will never achieve his dreams as soon as the obstacle presents itself. And what is called "education" results from a collective premise, so that children do not learn at the same speed and at the same level, and the parental educational role is sometimes complicated, because parents have not necessarily learned what is currently taught in schools, thrown into working life very early and knowing only the school on the street, bartering and friends with little nod to open a cultural book.

the child finds himself trapped in his difficulties without anyone being able to really help him, because he lives in a social and cultural climate from birth, where he learned that he would undoubtedly become like his parents, or that his dreams of grandeur will become inaccessible.

Do you really believe that your thoughts belong to you? At least not entirely, because they are just a pale copy of what you have been taught.

Whether it's Nietzsche, Kante, or other philosophers with tartar sauce, you don't necessarily think like them, why do I say that? And where do you think these philosophers got their teachings from? It didn't fall from the sky. They had their masters, and they just interpreted what they learned, and like everyone else, they were attached to icons. This means beyond that that we are all prisoners of a context of life.

I do not pretend to have infused science, far from it, but in the end, who owns it?

Why does a human being in most cases want to be right about everything? We have all found ourselves at least once in this kind of situation where your interlocutor seemed to make a bug, to hear you without listening to you, that is to say that each time you wanted to express an opinion, that it is concrete or not, whoever was in front of you dismissed it with the back of the hand without further ado.

All this seems childish on the part of your interlocutor, just to maintain the fact of being right, even if it is necessary to preach the false, and this is called stubbornness or a voluntary opposition of rejection, and there is the more often in individuals with a rather precarious social status, and who need this affirmation to exist.

Outside, the human being, as I have already mentioned, lives only by the image, the one we gave him and the one he gives himself, and there is something specific in each of us, the need for consideration and belonging to a group, and this is what I will address in a chapter upstream evoking the mass effect.

The origin of the icon goes back very far in the life of the being, it is located in childhood, this moment of relatively relative existence filled with glitter. We have the first images of our environment, of our parents, of our entourage in general, in the social condition in which you bathe, all this identifies the individual with a group (rich, poor, or modest).

The first images play a predominant role on our way of being and thinking, quite simply if you have from childhood, known the image of a house, a wealthy family, and the way of thinking of the 'entourage, you are an integral part of this environment whether you accept it or not!

Who remembers what he wanted to do in life when he was younger? To be a firefighter? Policeman ? Nurse? Strangely, almost everyone identified with these trades. But over time, all this has become utopian, why? Fear of not getting there?

No, not in all cases, it is only that for the most part, we follow the will of our heart, and life evolves with new desires. And I give it to you in a thousand, all this is fueled by our environment, yes yes, we are influenced, instrumentalized by the television media or magazines relating for example the heroic exploits of men and women who push us to become like these figures , what pushes us forward is this need for consideration fueled by our ego, this irrepressible desire to be raised in the Pantheon, in short, to become an "icon", this feeling of being loved for what we have become .

We all have this appetite and this thirst to succeed, to be a center of interest, without which, life no longer finds its meaning.

on the other hand, your conquering spirit has been forgotten, all because you were young, too fragile and naive, to believe everything that your entourage told you like "you have your whole life ahead of you!" (Very evocative of what I say there!), Because you needed benchmarks and you didn't believe in yourself, and you lived with this need to know if everything you were doing was right or wrong in asking the opinion of those around you therefore unwise themselves.

I imagine you, your eyes lit up with enthusiasm being younger, with your father or mother as your only support. You needed them to know where to go, but they could only give you elusive answers, not knowing for themselves what was best for you. What motivated and propelled you was the urge to move forward in your dreams.

But life has provided you with vain answers, and what I mean by that is all this pattern that you had then consummated thanks to or because of these images, like "you will not be able to do it!" "Or" put your feet back on the ground! "

also, the environment plays its role, making you gradually aware and by evolving in this world thus created, of your social condition, and of belonging to it in spite of everything.

What many have missed is the desire to fight, to act with their heart, to thirst for success, living in this universe too contrasted between dream and reality, between what others have, and what you own yourself.

In this reality, we are aware of this insurmountable mountain, submerged in latent doubts, pushing us to give up, all this with the circumstances preventing us from believing in ourselves.

*One hundred and one thousand faces*

*Watch the passage*

*Legs and arms crossed*

*The leader's glow*

*Blind the sleepers*

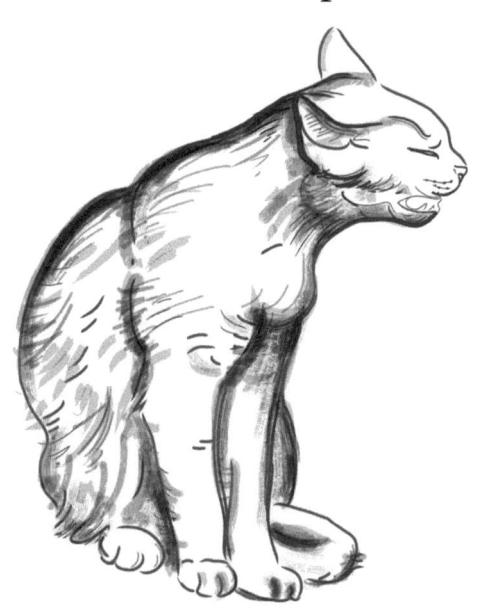

## STEP 4:
## *The judge*

*"In forecasting, judgment is superior to intelligence. Intelligence shows all the possibilities that can occur. Among these possibilities, judgment discerns those which are most likely to be realized."*
*(Gustave Le Bon / Yesterday and Tomorrow)*

*I thought long and hard about what the child had told me. Who was this judge? And why had he removed the creative genius from each being?*

*As I walked away from the child, my path seemed increasingly dark, and with each step I took, there was an impression of being observed, mocked, criticized, everything around me was only murmurs in this near darkness. Like hundreds of people saying discouragingly:*

*"You were not made for that! "*
*"Drop it ! "*
*"Stop dreaming ! "*
*"You're too bad for that!" "*

*These words revived old pains that I thought were forgotten, but in the end, they were sneaky, well hidden, creating like obstacles to the least of my words and gestures.*

*Then, all of a sudden, I saw it, what looked human was the merger of the sum of all my fears, those that manifested as I grew up.*

*So he was the judge, an entity that I myself created through my thoughts and false beliefs, it is because of this odious character that I have lost so many years. I felt it, it was in me, but what I saw accentuated my fears, how was I going to approach it?*

*He kept creative genius under his yoke, torturing him with false beliefs. This judge was despicable, constantly telling him that his ideas were stupid and that no one would validate them.*

*The closer I got to him, the more apprehensive I was, my heart was racing. There was a monster in front of me, and the poor creative genius frozen and hypnotized by his words of discouragement.*

*So I say to creative genius "Don't listen to him! this is what gives it more strength!"*

*He replied, "I can't! It's stronger than me!"*

*I say, "You are the only one who makes him strong! Stop listening, listen to me instead!"*

*Creative genius: "What do you want and who are you?"*

*And to tell him good things he's never been used to, I say to him:*

*"I am the one you helped to become stronger, I am your future, and the judge is nothing without your beliefs! You are the only master of your life and your actions! Repeat after me ...... it does not exist! .......he does not exist ! ......he does not exist !..... "*

*At that time, the creative genius plugged its ears and kept repeating "It doesn't exist! ....... he does not exist ! ...... he does not exist !.... "*

*At the same time, I said to him:*

*" You are the best ! The strongest, and you are the only master of your choices and your life! You have control over your destiny, but out of pity! Don't listen to it anymore! "*

*While continuing to speak to him and encourage him, I saw the judge become smaller, the sum of all my fears was reduced, and I felt it very quickly, my courage increased, and I saw the creative genius getting bigger and stronger and stronger, so that he had enough strength to bring the judge back to the ground. He had grown very small and fearful, like a frightened child.*

*As I saw the greater creative genius, everything was finally illuminated with iridescent colors, and everything seemed at hand, I could choose what I would like to see in this environment, my mind was able to create without no judge can say his word.*

*This world really belonged to me and all my choices were free. I just had to bring back the creative genius to the child, this other younger me*

You should never doubt the capacity of each being! Everyone has an innate talent for imagining and creating. They can change the daily lives of thousands of people, but they are blocked by the judgments, sometimes, of a single person, who decides their fate.

Not good enough, not clear enough, but also, not good enough, or not meeting his expectations.

In my opinion, a hidden talent needs to be encouraged, and it is not anyone who should prevent you! Whether it's race, religion, or the way we live, that's not what counts, it's the expression of his talent. What I regret is that the world is teeming with dormant spirits, having lost all their illusions, because of judgments without great values.

But some manage to get around obstacles to express all their talents, as was the case with a man named Korla Pendit.

He lived in the United States, and was known as a Hindu pianist who had his own style of music, by launching the musical genre called "exotica", very appreciated in the 1940s.

It must be said that at the time, Americans liked everything exotic, and he tried his luck in bars by looking for a job as a pianist.

The success was resounding, and gained notoriety, producers quickly noticed him and offered to make him television. Shortly after, he had his own musical show and gained fame all over the United States. He was acclaimed and achieved great success.

But there is another story ……

Korla Pendit, was not what he claimed to be! Indeed, two years after his death in 1998, his true identity was revealed. He was actually called John Roland Reed and he was not Hindu, but African-American, and the living conditions were terrible for people of color, especially in the 1940s, there was very little chance, even very thin, let his dreams come true, being judged by his skin color only for his talent. Peoples was slammed the door several times in the nose, but he got around the problem by taking on another identity.

We believe we decide! But we make no choice in all soul and conscience, our mind being programmed to follow stimuli which come from the outside world. In reality, we are all manipulated, by the media, the radio, the newspapers, and we follow a form of dictate of the choices made in higher authority.

As in the story of Korla Pendit, the Americans followed the mores of their time, following the mass effect, and failing not to follow the same path as these very dear little preprogrammed robots, the refractories are thrown in pujilat , and designated as traitors of the nation, pariates.

Ask yourself this question! what made the Americans love India and hate African Americans? "The Icon", but not only in the form of an iconic character, but also by influencing through the neuro-emotional association, by showing the most beautiful and the ugliest.

Unconsciously, the human being is influenced, even in the advertisement which adds its little watered-down touch, by using beautiful colors, beautiful decorations, or sometimes, a handsome man or a beautiful woman.

You will understand, everything is done to seduce the human, those responsible for communication by image knowing by heart human nature.

And going back to the judges, they have real power of life and death over humans, they can, make you, reader friends, guilty or innocent, counting on popular unrest. And if I hadn't made certain choices myself, if I had given my destiny to what I call "a judge", I would never have been a bestseller.

Trust yourself more, and awaken your creative genius! Find a way to show your talent, without having your fate in the hands of one person.

Also, do not always believe what we show you, a judge can take a lambda person, without really pleasing you, but they will put forward a whole panopli of artifices, showing the sensational, the extraordinary, such is the job of communication officers. That of pleasing what you don't necessarily like.

So take a step back from what you are shown and trust the most what you feel!

\*\*

*Rule n°3*

*Trust more
to yourself than to others*

\*\*

*"Lata sententia judex*

*Dessinit esse judex »*

*The retreat of the divine*

*Make room for the sovereign*

*The Victorious gives way to the Prudent*

## Step 5:
## Creative genius

*"Creativity is a flower that flourishes in encouragement but that discouragement often prevents it from blossoming."*

*(Alex F. Osborn)*

*I finally interacted with creative genius and told him that someone would be very happy to see him again. It's about the child, this other me who suffered because of this dream-breaking monster.*

*He told me that he had been waiting for me for a very long time and thanked me for having freed him from the grip of this moral, social, psychic hell that we call "judge", this unhealthy being who crossed the ages and which has adapted to the context, both at school, in high school and in professional life.*

*The one who said "no" to all the projects that this creative genius suggested to innocence. But the one who was believed to be strong was nothing more than a weak, it made you believe in a pseudo frailty, how you were unable to advance in life. Did you really need his advice to succeed, or was it more important to rely on yourself and your creative genius? In reality, you did not know anything about it, because human nature, in most cases, needs this feeling of power towards others to finally hide a form of impotence, and this is what we find in the narcissistic pervert.*

*My enthusiasm has grown since the judge was beaten. It was like a breath of air so powerful that I was breathless, and felt like I wanted to go ahead, to look straight at the horizon. And the one who had become free gave me a unique key for each individual, and he told me that when the time came, I would need it.*

*This key will open a door, but it was up to me to find out which one, and he told me that I have always known access. I put a string on this key and I wore it as a pendant, and when the time comes, it will reveal this truth, the one I have been waiting for a long time.*

*Then he took me down a corridor, a kind of gallery where several works, those of my life, were on display. Sometimes a firefighter, sometimes a police officer, I relived my youth and my future projects, and on each canvas, there was an inscription that concealed my face. These portraits had inscriptions.*

*"You will never get there!" "*
*" It's impossible ! "*
*"Do not even think about it ! "*
*.... etc .....*

*Then he showed me an access, the one where all my memories were locked up, and on entering, I found this child, smiling and grateful. And what was his reaction to his creative genius, the reunion with an old friend but it is not of this friend of which speaks this book ..... you will find out soon enough.*

*There was like a bright light, something sparkling lit my face, and it was my awakening. It was daylight and my eyelids were getting used to the soft and brutal gleams of this morning, and for the sun, it was time to point its rays.*

*My wife slept by my side, and I hastened to write down my memories while they were still fresh, because I was writing a book, and I was inspired by my dreams. The only problem is that I no longer remember the title of the book I saw in a dream ..... The leader alive? The leader give? .... The leader..... The leader ...... damn! I don't remember, but it will come back to me very quickly ..... I hope so ...*

There is a key that opens a door, and what is behind us is intended, like the most precious commodity, a treasure hidden in a safe, and it takes great patience to send so- even to find out what is hidden there.

During our lifetime, we have been hidden from the truth about our inner nature, imbued with discouragement and bad intentions. If only life had decided otherwise, who would we be?

We were badly advised from an early age, or in phase with false judgments, which made us doubt our real capacities. And this dreamy youth was murdered, in small or large doses. These wounds which do not show themselves, but which we feel, and therefore we feel incapable of changing, of choosing who we are, but what we have become are disjointed puppets.

The human mind is malleable and weak, and we live with this illusion of inner strength, because we have been manipulated by "judges". Treacherous and without morals, wolves disguised as lambs, and advancing in life, we no longer trust, But ...... too late! The damage has already been done, and the saddest thing is that no one has noticed it.

Also, it remains to differentiate the ignorant who has been educated by the judges, and who himself transmits to the next generations. He is an unconscious compared to judges, who knows what he is doing.

Where have our dreams gone? They have died out over time, because we have become beings without control of our existence. we all wanted (or almost) to exercise trades like firefighter or police officer, also, nurse or princess for the girls, and then, we changed, always in the hope of succeeding in our life, but with wear, we become deprived of our creative genius, making us short little formatted robots to follow only the dictates of a very selective society, not seeing talent in you, just one more manpower in the system. Clearly, you are not valued at your fair value.

However, I can tell you only one thing to close this step, when it comes to controlling your existence, you always have.

I talked about "patience" a little earlier, and that's the theme of our next step, the one that leads us to what is called the master of time.

*Lost in the four winds*

*Let light pierce its lance*

*Lutece is residence*

*Its lighthouse is in its lands*

*Pious than fair but little named*

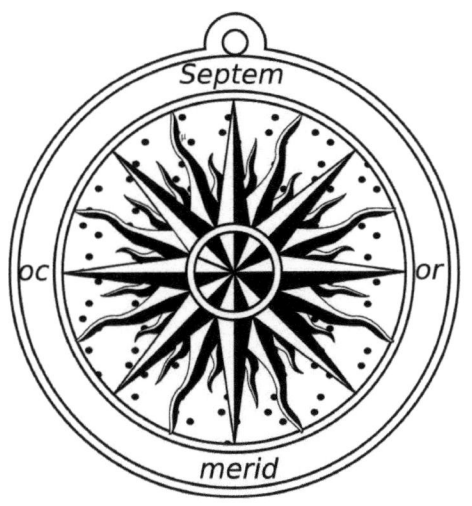

## Step 6:
## The master of time

*"Clocks kill time. Time is dead as long as it is driven by small cogs. When the clock stops, only time comes back to life."*

*(William Faulkner / Noise and Fury, 1929)*


*At 10:37 a.m., I was still on my notepad filling in pages as I remembered, and something had changed, I felt more inspired than before.*

*Since my encounter with creative genius, everything has been different. As if the life I led was not mine, and that I could take control of another while remaining in this same body. It was possible for me to redefine the beauty of ugliness and I gradually learned to appreciate. What is a moment? It is a precious commodity to which we must be very careful, and therein lies the real power, every second we can change our life, with each choice we make, with our breaths and our words, we become at any moment.*

*Are these lines real or are they from your fertile mind? Perhaps it is your imagination that invites you to become the creator.*

*But I didn't have time to finish taking notes that the doorbell rang. I hastened to write down key words on a piece of paper, a sort of memory aid that was just a sticky note on a corner of the table. I took my keys and went downstairs to see who I have the honor of visiting.*

*Arriving at the entrance, I saw a person I knew well, he was part of the UNC (National Union of Combatants), of which I have been a member for a few years. He was waiting for me with an envelope in his hand, and said:*

"Hello Yoann! I hope you are well, I have come to bring you an invitation for an exhibition which will take place in April next year in Cluses. "

Y "Hello Louis! I'm doing well, and you ? There are still a few months left for this, and what does this exhibition consist of? "

"This is an exhibition on a personal development author who has made his mark in the field and who has embarked on the creation of fantastic stories"

Y "You know Louis, I'm someone who's very busy right now, and I'm on a huge project, but I'll try to come! I would be happy to attend, and I would find a way to free him! "

Ok, if you change your mind, let us know! There will be a buffet and the mayor will be present. "

Y "Count on me, if there is a problem, I will call! Thank you for the invitation, see you very soon! "

I responded favorably to this invitation a few days later, and my partner would be with me. It took place at Place des Allobroges in Cluses. Almost everyone was present for this day. You couldn't go wrong, there was a large poster with the author's name written on it.

The author gave his books a curious name, he called them "his steps". It seemed so important to him to name them that way.

We were in this big room where it seemed to be crowded, some were chatting with each other, others were staring at books on shelves, a glass of sparkling wine in hand, and I discovered everything that this author had accomplished.

There was a key point to each of his books, and I started to think at this moment ..... a *moment as frozen in the past, because it endures thanks to its realization. And this moment gave birth to descendants, as a cause and effect phenomenon.*

*There were many titles on display, "The epilogue", "Viatorem", "The flea market ", "1802", and so many others ...... I thought to myself "This is the work of a lifetime that has had every moment! "*

*A single second was enough to have the click and create, and every moment, like a stroke of a pencil on a white sheet, traces of erasers and the wear of the keys of the keyboard that he used.*

*In fact, and what seems strange to say, the secret of success is that "Every time is all time!" ", And we use our time instead of using it to our advantage! And by following the example of the author, nothing can be built on its own and you have to be very patient. We should not seek success, even if that is what we want, what we have to do is to get down to it gradually.*

*The action in the moment is the fertilizer of success, and the more we stay in the present to "do", the more our universe is gradually built.*

*In this showroom, I was contemplating the books and I stopped on one in particular. The title was "Viatorem", I opened it to read a few pages, and I stopped at the height of a passage which spoke of a farmer and another character whom I knew very well, I read his adventures which was going to take him to the guardian of the temple.*

We are not the masters of passing time, but of what we do with it! And it unfolds before us at every step we take, at every choice we have, and it is now that makes the way of tomorrow.

Stop chasing time and live in the moment! There is so much to explore, because you ignore the value of a second, and anything can happen right now, somewhere in the world, in a second, there is the beginning of a birth, the end of a life, a war can be declared, an opportunity presents itself to you, but this precious second, it disappears as quickly as it appears.

It is possible to control our destiny if we learn to know the value of a time, of the space of a breath, but the human being lives with hope, this uncertainty of a speculated future, you all and all this gift, that of supposing, but we do not plant seeds in evasive possibilities, we do it in effort, in action, and by following all that is in movement, just like the needles of 'a watch.

We must live fully in the present moment, and not take refuge either in the past if we want to change our lives, or in the future, which does not exist yet. and to come back to hope, it unconsciously corresponds to future expectations. Do you hope to have when you have what you want? For example, you have a gold watch, it is yours, do you hope to have this gold watch? There is no longer any need to do it! when you are really in the present moment, there is no hope.

Each action is equivalent to a time, and we build our lives with each of these precious seconds, in this instant, this hinge between the past and the future.

That is why when you have projects in mind, there is no point in chasing the future, and being what you are not yet. And as the famous fable of the Fountain says, there is no point in running, you have to leave on time!

Also, stop living in the past, because what you are is not the past, but the present moment, this opportunity to be able to change everything in your existence is here, in this moment. And be aware that what was no longer and what will not be yet, and it is at this very moment that you can say "I am".

*Stick laid, ferris horses*

*Crossing path, race stopped*

*The walking man waits*

*Screaming steel arriving*

*Courrone posed decorating*

## Step 7:
## The farmer

*"When plowing begins, the other arts follow.
Farmers, therefore, are the founders of
civilization. "
(Daniel Webster / Remarks on the
Agriculture of England - January 13, 1840)*

*The passage of the book that I had in my
hands began thus ......*

*We were still at this exhibition, me and my
partner, and we were chatting with the
guests about the author. Who was he really?
It retained this element of mystery, and the
keystone of this story had long since been
surpassed.*

*After this day and an evening at the
restaurant, we returned home. My notepad
was still on my desk and I had collected quite
a bit of information that gave me new ideas.
It was only words, pieces of sentences, which*

*end to end tell a beautiful and magnificent story.*

*I began to write down as the adventures progressed, and I let myself be guided by my inspiration, as long as the point of my pencil coated each drop of ink on the thin white sheet. And I started to count on these terms ........*

*On the way to these countries, I met a farmer. He was advancing with a stick, his flock not far behind.*

*Y "Hello Mr. Farmer"*

*F "Good morning, foreigner! What is this meeting worth to me on my way? "*

*Y "Maybe you could help me, I'm looking for my way to find the guardian of the temple! "*

*F "Oh great God no! You are not a young man there, it is not the right way, because this is mine! But I would love to have your company on the way!"*

*Y "Leading to where dear friend? isn't it early to go to work?"*

*F "You are not there my friend, it is in my nature to beat the ground and to lead cattle, and there is no other hour to do my work! I am a farmer who as I call myself is an early bird! And why are you looking for the guardian of the temple?"*

*"There is a quest that I must complete, because the author is writing these lines that will lead me to my destination! And where does your path lead?*

*F "to a distant country, where my cattle will be at the end of their lives, without seeing anything else before! And this temple that you covet, on this path that you follow to accompany me is only one of the thousands that can lead you there!"*

*Y "Your cattle are going towards their end without knowing another destiny?"*

*F "Everyone has a destiny, without ever changing it, mine is to drive, this cattle which cannot flee!"*

*"What should your cattle flee from?""*

*F "the fatal end, a sad fate, that to perish without comfort, to know a different destiny which is not dedicated to them!"*

*"Are you taking your cattle to the slaughterhouse?""*

*F "Alas yes! What else do you want him to do? From birth, they are condemned, and if it is not by choice, but to be born bad, cattle it is, intended is programmed!"*

*Y "You say he has no choice but to follow this path to the abbey? So they are not free to flee, and can only stay, until the end of their hour which will ring?"*

*What is freedom Young man? Do you feel free? Imprisoned in the head of an author who traces the lines of your destiny, did you choose this adventure? I don't think so, but what is certain is that you are on the right track! I invite you to follow me with my cattle!"*

*Y "I have not chosen my destiny, nor my reality, I am just stuck between two worlds that an author has condemned me, but what is certain is that I do not think I will follow you further! It's time for me to leave you! I understand your way of thinking, but I don't want to follow it! Have a good trip!"*

*F "very good young man, and if you are looking for the guardian of the temple, the path is not very far, you are closer than even thought can perceive it without a great openness of mind! Go in search of the lair of the soul and you will know where your destiny will be! Good road to you my friend!"*

*Having left the short-lived farmer who was only doing his job, without any other judgment, I left! How sad it is to think that we are stuck in one destiny, that it is sad to know only fate, without fighting or trying, in effort and never giving up, with willpower. Beat the earth to work, this farmer knows the effort of a committed life, even if what he does not displease, but he is a farmer, and he loves what he does!*

*Do not judge without knowing what the advancing man is going through or has gone through! Each person has a role to play, but not the one we have been chosen for, but the one we love to do!*

*As for livestock, everything seems to have no way out for him, just a single destiny chosen for him, and the role he plays does not please him, or he does not know where he is going!*

*How sad to ignore your abilities, not to choose where to go, not to know where to end, in such a situation, there is no freedom, it is submission in ignorance and a chosen path by others.*

*And continuing to look for my way, I thought about it for a little while, but very quickly, I was going to find myself facing a wall that is not made of bricks.*

In the diagram that I propose to you now, there are two alternatives, to fight or to resign oneself, but bad habits have the hard tooth, for example, to vomit on the government and on the successful people, and to make you a confession , this is what these people who control you hope to keep you in this state of dissatisfaction in everyday life. Keeping or condemning everyone in their place.

This forgotten being, drowned in an agglomerated image spends more time making comparisons between us and the one who manages to create a life for himself. We are therefore more likely to subconsciously hate what we are than to love what we want to become, making us system dependent.

And this is so ingrained in you, that for most of you will become fully aware of the reality of these lines and will say "I act", others will prefer to keep blinders seeing only what they want to see, like a draft horse seeing only the possibilities in front of him, just a dirt road and nothing else.

Perhaps there is greenery, trees, flowers, and many riches that nature offers us, but despite everything, and being blind on each side of the blinders, the objective will always remain to go all right if he doesn't react.

it's a metaphor for what's going on in us as we continue on our dirt road. This is the road that many follow and each step represents a year without seeing what is on the sides, unexpected riches, hidden on each side of the eyes by blinders.

Stop for a moment and see the wonders of nature, just turn your head left or right to say

"Wow! it's beautiful, "and you just have to turn around to realize that we have missed many opportunities to see this lush nature.

Only, nobody stops, believing to be in the truth of their life, or after several years, alas! Too late, because the path leads to an abbey, just enough time to look one last time at the path behind you, everything that the being has gone through, and all the beautiful views that he missed, once the blinders were removed. He can see something beautiful and sad at the same time.

don't wait for someone to save you from your fate, she'll probably not come, only in rare cases where a brave person will come and challenge the farmer and finally take those blinders off.

Stop now and look around! Turn your head left and right and see what you're missing!

The magic thing about the human mind is that it can be influenced, but it's not the only trait it has, but I can assure you, everyone is, simply because we lack vigilance, because of multitudes of thoughts crossing our mind.

And ill-intentioned individuals can play on this, making us believe mountains and wonders in our daily lives, and those who work in communication know this by heart. Making us little robots of the consumer society, and falling asleep in beautiful promises playing the flute like sheep of panurge

The proof, is that since the beginning of this reading, you have not noticed it, but I give you a hint. If you look on page 113 (and it's not just on this page you will notice), you will see, hidden, the drawing of a ship. Have any of you been vigilant enough to check it out? it's crazy that you haven't seen it!

It reminds me of an interesting story that happened a long time ago. In 1887, in Newfield, Arizona, a man in his twenties named Will Campbell found a huge gold deposit. He extracted so much that he was able to shelter him and his family from the need, so much so that an article recounting his voluminous discovery attracted many people in search of the famous yellow metal.

Whole communities settled in this very rich place, at least, that's what they thought ....... Because this small town grew, attracting more and more treasure hunters. And all, leaving women and children at home, went to dig in the mines. Investors ate their hats as days, weeks and months passed to make way for years, as nothing but dust came out of the galleries.

Disappointed and having lost a lot, little by little, this city was emptying of its inhabitants, penniless in pocket ... .. and without gold. What happened then? To come back to this article, it was a ploy to repopulate the city. Why ? The idea came from a wealthy businessman by the name of Steve Garvay who promised a very large sum of money to a modest family to make believe that a gold deposit had been discovered.

It was very simple, Steve Garvay entrusted gold nuggets already extracted (it was easy for him to get them), to the father of the family, who had to pretend, by rolling in the dust to look more credible in front of the locals, enthusiastic, he contaminated the locals with his joy at having found gold (in reality, the enthusiasm came from the fact that a rich businessman had entrusted him with gold nuggets).

The press hastened to the affair, with many questions to ask, and an article later with cover photo launched the affair.

Guess who were the lucky winners? Steve Garvay and this modest family, they got rich, how? Steve, in front of the multitude of settling communities, was investing in shops and the local Saloon, he had become owner of these places by planning what he would do with them, and more people arrived in the city to look for gold, the better it was for his activities, and to reward this family, he gave them, in the form of contribution, tons of gold, which gave them more credibility ... ... they never talked about it ...... .until in 1932, a few minutes before his death, Will Campbell, who had become very wealthy, confessed this sinister story to the priest.

All this to explain to you the phenomenon of mass effect and it takes very little to trigger a craze for a situation that everyone would like to experience. And ill-intentioned individuals have understood this very well, and know how to play it very well, they are capable of creating situations to enrich themselves, and to return to our little story, it does not stop there!

The town of Newfield had gradually fallen into disrepair, no one wanted to hear about it anymore, because it was synonymous with great misfortunes, having hurt whole families who became ruined, but something happened, and this city was soulless living until spring 1958.

Anton McLory, a treasure hunter, had made up his mind to collect gold in these valleys. He had come from far away, and having read this story of discovery of gold on a very old article (the one cited more upstream), he did not know the rest of it, in particular the big scam of Steve Garvay.

The inhabitants of the neighboring cities took him for a fool, but they said to themselves that in the end, he did nothing wrong, because indeed Anton suffered from a psychological retardation and lived in his world, in short, it was a simple of spirit.

We let him do it, under the mockery of passers-by knowing the fate of these lands, "He will find nothing!" "They said!

But the most dangerous thing is that he was allowed to handle dynamite, and very precisely, on this afternoon of April 16, 1958, a blast made the windows of houses vibrate to neighboring cities.

The first reaction of the locals was to go see what was going on, some went by van to the place of the detonation. A huge cloud of dust screened, you couldn't see anything more than 20 meters away.

When the dust cleared, the locals found Anton lying on the ground, but he had nothing, just sounded by the explosion. But the most worrisome was the smell of diesel fuel, and it was covered in a dark substance, and some quickly realized that what Anton had discovered was an oil deposit.

In this world, there are many riches that ordinary people cannot see because they are dominated by unfounded rumors or based on old stories, and we as simple as we are, we base our beliefs on it.

The best thing about it is that we end up believing it hard as we are shown. Playing with our excess of confidence, and making us as fragile as children taking their first steps, tottering and hesitant, and I will also show you that I too am capable of handling some of you with disconcerting ease.

Indeed, I told you that there was a boat on one of the pages, and it is even a very large boat, you still do not understand?

Honestly, how many of you went to page 113? Do you have this overwhelming need to verify something for yourself just because I said it? And if you were really sure of yourself, you wouldn't have gone to see! But this was just a heat up, and there are professionals who can make you believe anything.

So be careful! Do not always believe what you are told or shown, appearances are sometimes misleading.

*Beware unhappy*

*Four accompany him*

*But only he will pass shortly*

*From the mountains*

*The guards are at the entrance*

## Step 8:
## Philosopher

*"If the philosopher is not happy, he is not really a philosopher."*
*(Roger Fournier / Diary of a newlywed)*

*I stopped for a moment to see where I was precisely because my destination took me straight to a wall, and that's not just a way of speaking.*

*Before him there was a man, a glass in his hand contemplating this wall. I wondered why he looked at him like that. So I went to meet him:*

*Y "Hello my friend, excuse me for interrupting you in front of the admiration you have for this section of wall, but I ..."*

*(He interrupts me)*

P "Your friend? Who do I have the honor to speak to at this moment? After the rain, the good weather comes!"

Y "My name is Yoann and I am looking for the caretaker, and it is my turn to ask you the same courtesy to know who you are!"

P "I am what I am and this since the world is world"

Y "And why do you contemplate this wall?"

P "I'm looking for a way to get to the other side, but obviously, it's impossible! What do you want? it's life!"

Very intrigued, since the wall in question was only a section of barely three meters wide, I pointed out to him, but very quickly, this character retorted sharply:

P: "How dare you claim to know better than I young man? I'm the only one who knows *what you're not supposed to know! Because you think you know, and who better than I can know? The world is like this!"*

*Y: "It falls on the meaning! If you go around the wall, you can... ..."*

*(He interrupts me a second time)*

*P "What do you think I am currently doing? I know what I have to do, and I'm someone who goes ahead! Everyone sees noon at his door!"*

*Y "For the moment, your front is leading nowhere but to the wall"*

*P "And that's why I'm here, because it's at the foot of the wall that you can see the wall better!"*

*Y "And why do you make ready-made sentences? ... .. since the world is world ... ...*

*this is life ....... The world is thus made ... ... everyone sees noon at their door ... ... . "*

*P "This is not how you say young man, you are wrong! We say Since the world is THEEEE world, it's THEEEE life, the world IIIIIS thus made ... .. "*

*"Is that what I just said to you? "*

*P "Would you dare to contradict me? I know I'm right, and who sows the wind picks up the storm! "*

*Y "So, I let you find the solution all by yourself! "*

*P "that's it! You take offense for nothing! I will listen to you for the solution, and you will see for yourself that I am right. But don't sell the bear skin before you kill it! "*

*With these words, I went with him to the other side of the wall, but showing me the back of the wall, he said to me:*

*P "You see? We cannot go further! There is always a wall, and two holds is not worth one you will have it!"*

*Y "But it's the same wall"*

*P "Of course, what did you believe? I had already thought about this possibility, and there is no way out, The world is like this!"*

*Y "There is absolutely no way to have a dialogue with you!"*

*P "And what do you think we do like now? Do not put the cart before the horse!"*

*A little nervous, I said to him:*

*Y "you are right!"*

P "You know young man? I have something to teach you! We were all born on the day of our birth, and time is counted in hours, and rain is not good weather! "

Y "Why are you telling me something I already know? "

P "Because I need to feel that I exist and that I am important! We must separate the grain from the chaff! "

Y "No wonder you are alone, impossible to exchange points of view, always in a critical spirit, always to contradict, to expose your science believing you the best, to teach me what I already know, and your sentence ending in parables, would someone support you in these conditions?

P "It is you who are always critical and who contradict me! Who sows me wind harvests the storm! The world is like this! It's life ! "

*Y "I leave you facing your wall where you will go nowhere"*

*P "Very well, now leave me! I have to continue what I was doing, and you cut me off in my action! To pass the wall, it's on your left or on your right! When the moon rises, the sun sets! It's life !"*

*A bit irritated, I set off again towards my quest, it occurred to me the following inspiration, who better than a king can know his kingdom?*

During our lifetime, we face philosophers. I'm not talking about the real ones, but the kind of people who don't live in Stendal or Cendrare, but who have a very high opinion of the world as if they were the ones who designed it!

These philosophers, we meet them everywhere in our daily life, these individuals who say they go everywhere, but who go nowhere, and all my life during, I met, and I still continue, these people without flavor, with whom he is impossible to exchange anything, always to believe oneself superior to others.

These same people who make my good fortune on these lines, a very common human typology who feel lived, but who do not breathe it.

They are often, unfortunately, their own victims in this case, because their fatalistic spirit finds itself facing a wall they have built, and cannot see other fields of possibilities than those they have set for themselves.

They take refuge in their social condition, having only as real references to Desproges or Colucci, and who believe themselves to be the kings of the world by having read only very few books by true philosophers.

These same who explain the meaning of life without knowing how to improve their own. They have a very strong mental conditioning that even if they read a few pages (by miracle) of a famous author, they would still find to contradict.

They are genuinely closed minds, limited, who often find themselves alone. For them, the problem is opposite and it is impossible to get around it. They don't listen to people and there's no point in helping them.

Precisely, it's like talking to a wall.

This kind of individual make philosophy that does not use the school bench, but the cobblestones, they have a very narrow vision of the world and are not thirsty to know more than true philosopher, to to say that we must dig deeper into the knowledge, and not to repeat stupidly what we can read in the books, swinging from Plato to all sauces.

What made me an author? Just because I mention it there now? Not at all, what made me an author is "the effort", which means that I worked hard and long to achieve this result, a lot of doubts and questions, many questions about what I was going to do to get there, hours of writing, reflections, sometimes in painful conditions.

What pushed me towards personal development and human nature? These subjects interest me more than ten years ago and they came naturally, and you know how? With what I have already gone through in childhood, as well as in adulthood, I experienced difficulties as a young person, to undergo rejection by others, but over the years, and also thanks to many readings on the subject of personal development, I learned how to gain this confidence which I missed so much!

Because of this, all that I suffered in mockery, in criticism that weakened me psychologically, I made of it an instrument, that of my inspiration, not by learning from others, but from myself. What made my weakness in the past, I made it a strength, and I admit that the more I am criticized, the more it inspires me, and it was very useful to me in the sense that I became a bestseller ...... .by learning from human nature. In fact, I had everything at my disposal to succeed and the human by his inappropriate arrogance continues to do it for me, give me something to grind, and I love it! And if I had to say something to those who criticized or mocked me, it would be ...... A BIG THANK YOU!

Human nature teaches me a lot, and I think that many of you should be inspired by it rather than suffer from it, because you are better than them, in the sense that those who criticize you are in a few kind, weak. No courage, no motivation, just a critical sense and mockery, nothing more. But don't ask them to try to get out, they won't, because they're afraid to get out of their comfort zone, they're afraid of "it looks like ... "Paradoxically, they like to criticize, but are afraid of being.

Also, not to say that badly, because what I am talking about is only a case in point, human nature fascinates me by its diversity, because I find that we have a lot to learn from it. Both down to earth and fatalistic as constructive (well! Constructive, the word there too is to be enjoyed in all ways!).

I also learned that human nature can be seriously mistaken and some prefer to persevere despite everything in error, to their relentlessness to see only what they accept as true or false without any other form of trial, and without seeking to see beyond the other possibilities the world offers. For them, "it's like that and it should stay like that! "

Which brings back to these counter philosophers, these "rare birds" (not so rare as that!), To which all sciences are acquired, by ruling out the possibility that they may be on the wrong track. As trapped in the illusion of truth, in a cell of utopias, and outside this cell, a whole universe of possibility that they cannot see, and yet everyone holds the key to these geoles that we are building ourselves !

But the sage is the one who knows that there is still a long way to go to ultimate knowledge, even though it does not exist! Why ? Because the universe of possibilities is vast and infinite, and the wary and realistic man only explores its beginnings, he is in the embryonic phase of knowledge!

the human being in his mind conceives a ready-made idea of the world, to say to himself that reaching his objectives is "impossible", that we are destined to follow only one path, well aligned, like a herd that the we lead to the abbey, and if the absolute consciousness of being showed us all the possibilities, the human being, in his effort and his thirst for discovery would evolve again and again!

Which is a great pity, because observation made and we do not know why, the man stops advancing to adulthood, it is these fatalistic side to say that in any case it is too late and that we must accept his sad fate without fighting? Is it that sense of assertiveness to say that as an adult, we need to know everything? Or was he influenced for a long time by the outside world? (friends, family, colleagues, etc.).

The word "IMPOSSIBLE" should never exist, it is what kills the human dream and its realization, it is what prevents it from saying "why not?" I should try this! "

what blocks the human being is that he says to himself that in any case, he will fail, but he forgets that no victory, or no success is possible without this element, and all the great authors like Robert Kyosaki will tell you!

By accepting that we could be wrong, instead of getting stuck in the "it is not for me! " all realization is done in failure and perseverance, everything is possible in action and restarting, and it takes certs to have a good dose of courage and determination to get there!

Who has never experienced pain? Who has never known doubt? Who has never thought of giving up on all those who have achieved the coveted glory?

man has been influenced for a long time by the outside world, his mind has been so manipulated in his social condition, so much has been drummed on this word since childhood.... "IMPOSSIBLE", and the adult man undergoes, gives up, accepts, a philosopher on life without really knowing it, but in all this, there is one thing that he does not do, it is to dream and to realize his dreams! How? 'Or' What ? By trying to hold on to it and accepting failure as the ally of its future success, then trying again and again forging your life in effort, and that's how we build an experience , by fighting and not by resigning oneself and becoming a down-to-earth false prophet.

And yet, there is a gateway to our dreams, that is the imaginary, in the creative and artistic sense of the term. Look at those who succeed, they work hard, have a vivid imagination, have drawn up their life plan, that of their dream. This little bit of madness that transforms the speculative static into reality.

it is to try without remaining frozen in community standards and to stop being conditioned like a wise little robot and to believe everything that you have been told, that you were null, that it was impossible, but is what have you observed everyone who told you that? Is their life better than yours? Are they successful? They have nothing but "blah blah ...." "(Do what I say and not what I do!".

it is only in the effort that one becomes bigger and stronger, act, give oneself experience, try, and not by letting oneself fall asleep by vain chatter, chatting or fabrication .

It takes a good deal of courage to persevere despite obstacles, and that's where you see the winner and the fighter. And acting does not have the same meaning as unnecessarily blablater.

As for counter philosophers, you will observe him uselessly lamenting the human condition, blocked by the same psychological wall, without bringing anything other than bottomless and lived chatter.

Avoid listening to them! Run away ! And surround yourself with people with whom it is possible to have a real dialogue with respect for all! And these will tell you that everything is possible and will encourage you to succeed, as I do, without distinction of belonging to a social group or other, the human being really ignores his skills and how far he can go if he don't try anything. And he must act according to his heart, not according to what he has been taught.

\*\*

## Rule n°4

*Act according to your heart
and not according to what you have
learned*

\*\*

*Aramon, Sarrians and Orgon*

*Cross the same horizon*

*Grandmaster, base is laid*

*Holding Ponant twenty eight cubits*

*No one to cross*

## Step 9:
## The king

*"To be king is silly; what matters is to make a kingdom. "*
*(André Malraux / The royal voice).*

*A huge city stood before me, held by a guard. How was it that he was the only one to watch over this gigantic kingdom?*

*I approached him to ask him to meet the king.*

*"Excuse me, I'm looking for a king and I would like to know...."*

*(he interrupts me)*

*G "Which one ?"*

*Y "Why?" There are several of them ? "*

G "We are all the kings of our own kingdom, by the way, I am myself!"

Y "But how is it that it is you who oversee this kingdom?"

G "Because no one else is capable of doing it, and yet they all proclaimed themselves kings, leaving the real king at the entrance of this one!"

Y "They made a mutiny and they kicked you out?""

G "It's more complicated than that! They appointed me king so that I could guarantee their security and their prosperity, but they chose to have control of the kingdom in my place, by making absurd decisions, and having no say in it. on the choices they make, just asking me to resolve their bad decisions!"

"Are they safe in there while you're taking risks for them?" Why ?"

*G "Because they assume nothing of what they do, they believe to be in the truth and cause me many problems with the neighboring kingdoms, the proof is, you are there! "*

*Y "how that? I have no kingdom! "*

*G "We all have our own kingdom, but it remains hidden for those who are not aware of it! And here, they all took refuge in mine, having desires of greatness and perstance, savoring the good moments of life, knowing absolutely nothing in the world, but loving to explain it! "*

*Y "Very good! But I did not come here to debate it, and I am only looking for the guardian of the temple! "*

*G "He's right in front of you!*

*Y "But I thought you were the king!" I'm a little lost, tell me who you are! "*

G "I told you! The guardian of the temple is me, but I am the great king of the kingdom of kings! "

Y "Impossible that you are the guardian of the temple!" "

G "You get it wrong young man! I am indeed the guardian of THIS temple! Yours, you will have to find it! "

"And how can I do it?" Which route should I take? "

G "you have obviously made a very long trip to get here, and I understand your eagerness to find what you are looking for, but rest assured, it is not far away, I would even say that it is much closer of you than you can imagine! But it is out of the question to let you enter my temple, because inside; everyone seems to have taken control of it, and I don't *want to be the guarantor of a new individual who is not looking for his own kingdom!"*

*"Can you at least show me the route to get there?""*

*G "subconsciously you know this road, for that reason I will not indicate it to you!"*

*Y "Why don't you want to tell me?"*

*G "You are a king, I told you! And why should I tell you something that only you know? This is what I find curious, everyone, even in my kingdom wants to make decisions, but not take the responsibilities that go with it! So they ask the guardian to watch over the kingdom, which is in peril of uncertain decisions!"*

*Y "You absolutely don't want to tell me anything? I'm wasting my time here, I really thought you could help me!"*

G "If you are looking for the guardian of your temple, you just have to go to the neighboring village, someone there can tell you, ask the magician, I met him recently, and he will help you in your quest »

Y "Thank you for your help, great king, and I hope that you will one day regain control of your kingdom! "

G "Hope is vain, everything is happening right now, and great king I am, guardian I will stay! I wish you luck in your young man quest! "

This meeting left me wondering, and in the end, who is the king of his kingdom? Is it possible to lose control of it? Does every decision we make endanger our destiny? And who is still able to assume his choices? I'm learning all the time in this adventure, and it's just beginning, because it's just the beginning, right now!

There are individuals who like to revel in their problems, and ask others to solve them for them, and yet they have everything to be happy, a job, income allowing them to make ends meet, and even to put money aside, but still they do not do! Why ? Because they prefer to spend their money in the wrong way, and then complain that they no longer have it.

Can we reason with them? As we often say, everyone is king in their kingdom, they are programmed in this way, and it is an endless circle. Sometimes it seems like they are doing it on purpose, or they are aware of it, but that despite everything, they do nothing to change their mentality.

This is part of one aspect of human nature that persists in error, but how to reason with an adult who is supposed to be responsible?

*On the top of the three valleys*

*Clues are hidden there*

*Treasures and coins, you will discover*

*If master of silence*

*Gives you the chance*

## Step 10:
## *The magician*

*"The universe is full of magic and it patiently waits for our intelligence to refine."*
*(Eden Phillpotts)*

*My story begins right now, but I don't know how it started. Everyone I encountered on my journey seemed very strange to me, and I was still far from imagining, if only I could "be", what fate awaited me at the end of this obscure journey?*

*Who am I really? A creator? A creation? the work of that fertile spirit that made me believe in the instant dream on earth? I didn't know it, all I had left was this truncated thought and a vulgar key that opened no door, or at least I wasn't aware of it yet.*

*Continuing on my way, I saw a remote village, and I wondered what kind of people I was going to meet again. But approaching me a little closer, everything seemed silent, and pushing the doors of the enclosure of this place, there were many agitations, of the villagers strolling hat holding and gentes accompanying ladies. Everything was well coordinated, each of the inhabitants with their usual task, walking or working, there was a baker, a butcher, the parish priest talking with a police officer, I felt like at the beginning of the XXth century.*

*To one of them in front of me, I asked the following question:*

*Y "Hello sir, sorry to interrupt your activities, but I am looking for the magician, and I was told that I will find him right here!*

*V "Oulah! Sacrebleu, if that's what brings you here stranger, you will find it in the tavern which is just around the corner, behind the fish merchant. "*

*Taking leave of this individual, I therefore headed for the tavern he indicated to me. I pushed open the door, and all eyes turned to me. And one of them said:*

V *"that's new! I'm pretty sure he's looking for the magician too! "*

*(and everyone laughed!)*

*"What's going on here? And why are you laughing?*

V *"My friend!" Excuse this teasing, but you are not the first to come here in search of the magician! it's almost become a habit here!*

Y *"Why do you say this? And what is this establishment? "*

V *"A tavern, don't you see? Look around! In your opinion, are we here to count the glasses? "*

*(laughs again... ..)*

*Y "Exactly, if it's a tavern, who tells you that I'm looking for a magician? Didn't you ask yourself if I was there just to quench my thirst? At least, what the brand tells me! Or am I on a committee of sellers with little jokes? "*

*(A silence settles!)*

*The tavernier asked me what I wanted to consume, and given the atmosphere, I was not going to be satisfied with a lemonade in this hilarious environment.*

*"I would take it like these gentlemen please!" "*

*T "Then, a beer for you! Excuse this slightly agitated reception, these men have consumed quite a bit, and it is rare to have visitors other than the regulars of this place! "*

Y *"Don't worry! I know this kind of establishment where those who come there do not come out very fresh! Can I tell you something?"*

T *"Go ahead!" tell me, and I already know your question, are you actually looking for the magician?"*

*"It is correct, but I do not wish to ask this slightly tipsy community!"*

T *"A little, you think? (Laughs) "If he's the one you're looking for, you'll find him in the village library!"*

Y *"The library? I have not seen a sign indicating this one! Where can I find it?*

T *"Haaa my friend! It has been unoccupied for ages, except of course by the only owner, but many souls live there, it is said to be haunted! this is the building that is several meters away, and you will recognize it! the place seems to be neglected, and nobody dares to venture there "*

*Y "The poor, he must feel good alone in this building surrounded by all these wandering souls. Thank you for your help ! How much do I owe you for beer? "*

*T "I offer it to you! You have come all this way to find the magician, it deserves a beer! That said, I wish you good luck, because many have tried and abandoned, for this reason my clients know this place well and those who have tried to venture there! "*

*After this exchange, I left the tavern, this place that I found much worse than what I was going to discover there. And now I was heading to the place indicated, that sinister abandoned library in which no one has ventured.*

*At the entrance of this one, on the ground, there was an inscription, leaves covered it, and with my foot, I spread these leaves, and I saw what it noted:*

*"This is not the magician's home, but you will find the path to him when you enter it! "*

*A rather obscure enigma that I had trouble solving, but wanting to know a little more, I decided to enter anyway, I pushed open a large, very old door, the creaking of which made me shiver with fear, as an indicator of this. that I was going to find there. the place seemed dark to me, lit just by the light of a candle, but who had lit it?*

*There were cobwebs everywhere, strange noises, as if I was not alone, and suddenly "boom" a book fell right in front of me, it seemed to come from very high, from the floors superiors.*

*B "who is there? Replied a sinister voice.*

*I froze suddenly and saw in the distance a man holding a candle, he was behind what looked like a wicket.*

*Y "Hello sir, I'm looking for the magician"*

*B "what is it then? Replied that voice which seemed to echo everywhere in the house! "Is it a book?" I know this title, do you have a library membership card? "*

*Puzzled, I asked him this question:*

*Y "A subscriber card? But this is the first time I have come here! "*

*B "come closer! Do not be shy ! Just fill out this subscription form, noting your details so that I can enter them into my database! "*

*I filled out this form and handed it to this man who turned to what looked like a dusty old PC who looked like it hadn't been used in ages.*

B "So! Mr MERITZA Yoann ...... .this says something to me ....... Hadn't you written a book a while ago called "The leader living".... "The life of leader ... ..hemm ....... what's the title already?

He searched his memory, head in the air and petting his goat, and I replied:

Y "The lead of life? "

B "Yes, that's it! it's an honor to meet an author like you right here! "

"Sorry to tell you this, but I haven't written any books!" "

B "And yet, I expected your visit, because it appeared in the pages of this book! But where did I put it away? "

"Sorry, but if you were waiting for my visit, why were you so surprised to see me arrive?"

B "Because it is only one story among many others, just a story of which we are the main heroes, and my memory fails me, to read all these books .... each one tells a story in his own way.

Y "It is very interesting what you tell me there, but it does not tell me where I could find the magician?"

B "I understood your question, young man, and what you are looking for is the title of a book! It is in one of the shelves of this library, but it is up to you to search for it, and you will give up as so many others have done, I am sure!"

Y "why do you say that?"

B "The magician is the title of a book, but it is not written on the cover, it has been hidden under another title that you should look for! Is that what you came for, right?"

Y "Yes, I understand dear sir, and you don't want to help me?"

B "Absolutely not! This is a quest that needs to be done alone, and I have no power over what you decide to do!"

Y "So I'm going to take my courage in both hands and try to find it! Pfiou! The task seems difficult to me!"

B "in this case, good luck to you my friend! And if you need me for something else, I'm here! You can ask me for tea, coffee and whatever you want, you might be here for a while! Anyway, I live here!"

Y "Thank you!"

*I was approaching the first shelf, and I was already sighing. Behind a ton of dust and in the company of spiders having made their nest, were works that I knew well! There were many authors, ranging from Dan Simmons, Rhonda Byrne, Stephen King for the most recent, to George Orwell, Florence Scovel Shinn, J, R, R Tolkien for the oldest. And there were also old books of science, math, philosophy, and nothing that told me where the magician was.*

*B "do not be discouraged dear friend! Shouted the individual who was now several meters from me! "Do you want some tea?" "*

*"Gladly!" Thank you very much ! "*

*while I started reading, the man I had met offered me a cup of tea. I was reading for hours now, dusting each of these books, that fatigue was being felt.*

*Y "I have to go to rest! I can not stand it anymore ! "*

*B "I warned you, it will not be easy! Sit on the sofa downstairs! I'm going to cook, wouldn't you mind joining me? You know ? I have very few visitors to this place! "*

*Y "Thank you very much! I'm willing to join you, and I've been reading for hours, it's been digging! "*

*We then ate together and he asked me this question:*

*B "did you find what you were looking for? "*

*Y "no, not yet! And it's quite misleading, because from what I've read so far, there is a real magic in each of his books that made me travel and discover new things, I learned a lot from each of them, and the authors of these books are true word magicians "*

*B "You are on the right track, but you have not found it yet! Look again, it will be where you least expect it! "*

*Y "What does that mean? that we still have to read several of these books?"*

*B "You will find it, if you can be patient! You know? You are like most people in search of immense power! They are in a hurry to find this magician, but he only shows himself to the one who really knows how to look for him!"*

*Y "I feel exhausted, and my head will explode, we will resume this conversation later, it is time for me to leave you! Thank you for the meal, I wish you a very good night!"*

*B "Do not thank me, it is quite natural, it is rather up to me to tell you for the company you give me! Good night to you dear friend, I'm going to resume my activities, and rest too!"*

*While I was resting, thousands of information were circulating in my mind, everything I had read gave me funny dreams, trips between Louis Ferdinand Céline and Romain Gary, these places in my imagination seemed strange to me.*

*In the early morning, I was awakened by a light that passed through the dusty windows of this building, everything seemed to be lit in the section that I had read the previous day.*

*B "hello my friend! Slept well? "*

*Y "Yes, it was fine, the sofa is comfortable, but I kept thinking about my reading from the day before! "*

*B "this is normal, because you have called the magician, and he begins to come towards you! "*

*I had coffee with this person, and we were discussing what I had read, he told me that this is only the beginning, but that I would manage to meet this magician.*

*I started reading where I left off! And the hours and the days passed, and the more I advanced in my research, the more the library seemed lit.*

*Several months had passed since I had started to read all the books in this place mixing the strange and the fantastic, and arriving at the end of my readings, without having yet found this magician, I only had left 'one book to read, and it was the one I wrote.*

*B "Did you find what you were looking for my friend? "*

*Y "No, still nothing! No magician! was that just a deception? Isn't he? "*

*B "I assure you that it does! Think carefully ! Where can we find the magician? In a library, right?*

*Arrived at the page of my book, evoking the discussion with the one who kept this library,*

*I had like a flash of lucidity, finally, this place, it was the cave of this magician, but we could not find it! I was looking for magic among these books and I found it, and that made me say that in the end, we are all magicians, those of knowledge and words. And we don't use this power enough.*

*The magician has always been with me...
..and in me, I was what I was looking for!*

You are not yet aware of the true power of this book and that which resides in each human being, and even if you pretend otherwise, let these lines reach their destination, and all your questions will be answered as to choice I made while writing these improbable texts you would say to me, but which have a deep meaning for the spirit in phase of awakening.

There is a real magic in each of us, and thanks to it, it is possible to transform our life, for the one or the one who really believes in it, because there is always a magician or a sorcerer at the bottom of our being.

Does anyone other than ourselves control our destiny? The answer will seem ambiguous if you still haven't understood who you are! Let me develop!

First, I would answer "Yes" in relation to the image (or "images") that we were given from childhood, through parental or school education, through social and professional. In fact, it is a subset of what we really are, a living being dressed in many costumes, those we did not choose when we were younger, the door was open to all forms of beliefs coming from others, but not by itself.

We have these images inside of us and these are the ones that make up most of our raison d'être, or at least that is what we believe.

In the second time, I would answer "No", we have no control over our destiny, the fact that what we like, did somewhere we have not been forced a little hand for the like ? Is this what our deep being wants? And in this, we have lost all of our identity in beliefs that are not in accord with our true nature.

I give you an example :

At the bottom of us reside two beings, one representing the good, and the other representing the evil, a magician and a sorcerer (you will understand later in these pages). The two are fighting a merciless war, one to dominate the other, but think carefully my friends, what is it that gives so much strength to these two entities?

These are our beliefs!

The ones that we have been taught right or wrong, what we let in or out of our soul, and very few people are aware of the real power that resides in each belief, and the world (yours) is made up of that way.

Imagine an individual who goes to consult a witch to cast a spell on a woman or a man for rather obscure reasons.

The latter made sure to grant his wish provided that he paid him the sum of € 5,000.

the individual did not honor his payment, the witch said these words

"You will know a lifetime of woe"

taking her word for it, a whole series of events happen in her life. Debts, family problems, unemployment, and he thinks he is in the grip of a bad spell, but subconsciously, it is he himself who gives him strength because of his beliefs, and he has returned to a form of vicious circle. And all events further reinforce these beliefs.

Then, he will then see an exorcist who will help him to free himself from this "bad luck", he thus gets rid of the form of curse which he was hostage, a whole series of blessed events happens to him by the after.

the human mind is a huge, very powerful generator that gives strength to beliefs

Beliefs have been the essence of this world since it existed, of the world we live in, and subconsciously, we give a lot of energy and impulse to what we believe to be true or false, as we go as we move forward.

You live in a prefabricated world and the consequences of what you believe are always up to your actions.

Look for the real magician who is in you, he has a very great power, that to change your life considerably, but the problem is that the human being evolves in a conditioned and hermetic society, believing himself free to choose, but in the bottom , what is a choice? There is none and you act according to the beliefs instilled. There is no misfortune or happiness, it is only you who are the creators. And you seem so locked in this world that you don't believe it at all, or however, you start to doubt and open your eyes!

Who are we?

You will have plenty of time to discover it over the pages and what will follow may surprise you!

*In its ember fortress*

*A great Celtic king lived*

*Visible from a breach*

*Of stones and bones, the light of day*

*Show the way to Odin*

## Step 11:
## The wise man

*"The wise man, without ever doing great deeds, accomplishes great things."*
*(Lao-Tseu)*

*By learning a little more from this "magician", I understood that I was never far from the temple where the guard was, but this journey through these pages was long, and I needed me sit down for a while to regain my senses.*

*All of a sudden a voice will be heard*

*S "Don't do this! It would destroy you!"*

*to that voice which seems so at once so close and so close I replied*

*Who's talking to me right now?"*

S *"Unconsciously, you know who I am! I am everywhere and nowhere, a soul who knows the truth you are looking for! Just like you, you know this truth, have used it, without ever knowing it!"*

*The replied rather puzzled*
Y *"What are you talking to me about?"*

S *"To regain your senses of course!"*

*Did I think so hard that this voice was heard? I didn't know how he did it, but my curiosity grew stronger than expected and I asked him:*

Y *"Why shouldn't I regain my senses?"*

S *"They are the ones you have rejected throughout your young man existence! The senses that have followed you all the time and to whom you have turned your back, but they made their presence known by waving in your thoughts!"*

*Y "Could you tell me a little bit about yourself? Because I admit being a little lost, you tell me that I know who you are unconsciously, but I ask you just to help me a little, because I try hard, I still do not understand!"*

*S "I am the one who allows us to dream and imagine a better world, the one who opens the doors to the invisible side of being for those who do not live in themselves, I am the pen, the paper and the ink, the essence of these lines, both creator and creation, but who of us created the other first?"*

*On these words, he gave me a book whose*

*title was somewhat disturbing, it was entitled "the lead of life", the same that you hold in your hands currently friend readers.*

*Y "What exactly is this book about?"*

*S "It is about your adventure, mine and that of our life with all, even that which arrives to decipher the lines of this work will open the doors of our spirit, and consequently, all will be possible if we take some all conscience"*

*"Do you know the author of this book?""*

*S "Basically, who is the author? You? Me? If my conscience dictates me to become the author, I will become it, one always becomes what one thinks of it!"*

*Y "What does this mean? I would like more response!"*

*S "From what you already know and what you are looking for, there is a very short distance between these two paths, there is a passage between these two worlds and I know this passage, do you want to finally discover your true nature ? "*

*On these words, the one I call "the sage", unless it was the author of this book who decided so, took me through a sort of tunnel, a very dark place where the dominant emotion was crossed to enthusiasm and fear of what I was going to discover there. And the sage accompanied me.*

*As I walked in the dark, a bright light came out, it was warm, reassuring, and in the distance I could make out a silhouette.*

*Something in me was soothed, and I asked*

*this distant form the following question*

*Y "Who are you?" I can't distinguish you! "*

*D "I am the being with a thousand faces, although I have more than 7 billion, the one who has several names, the pure and the divine, the alpha and the omega, the one who is named without knowing where he is, the one we are looking for, but who is still in his temple! But call me heavenly father if you want! "*

*Y "Are you God?" "*

*D "Everyone gives me different names, but if that's the one you chose, then I will be for you! "*

*Y "Perhaps you could help me in my quest, I am looking for the one who is called the guardian of the temple"*

*D "You still haven't understood? in this adventure, we are all the guardians of our temple, even the author of this book is aware of it, everyone waits for miracles, but I am the miracles which live in each of the human beings, and wait hoping for answers on my part, while everyone knows them if they could open their minds with what they have! "*

*As he walked closer to me, I saw someone who looked exactly like me, and I felt like I was in front of a mirror, he was such a true copy of me. And he said these words:*

*D "I am always like my neighbor and the reality is what you make of him as a young man. We are all creators and creations, I am portrayed in different ways, but the only real face that I have is the one that is in every being. The truth will be revealed to you if you learn who you are! "*

*With these words, he showed me something that I had kept for a long time, what he or we all call faith, and each individual has that faith on a small or large scale. So I took what he was showing me, this object hung on my necklace like a pendant ...... it was a key, and he said to me:*

*D "Now you know who you are and who you are looking for! So open that door! "*

*Y "I don't see any door"*

*D "It is because you do not see it yet, but I will show you the access that opens up to the depths of your being!"*

*With these words, And telling me my heart, I*

*understood that it was the door, I entered the key in the lock, and from that moment, I had reached a new stage, that of spiritual awakening.*

At the beginning of this book, I warned you that it would take on a whole new dimension, and you understand better why I said that I was not the author of this book.

The reality is this: we are all what we want to be and not be, the guardians of our own temple. And the key opens the door to an infinite world between real and imaginary.

And what I would like you to understand, what the others are, we are all unconsciously, at the same time authors, actors, creators and creations, but what stimulated us the spirit of false beliefs made us of beings existing only through images and we only reproduce what we have learned.

What we are in the end, we believe to be, but we are not!

We are all looking for something and we are all hoping for it, but where the hope is, there is no faith, and they cannot both live in one place.

The hope lies in the lack, the need and the expectation that someone or an event will bring it to us, while faith opens the doors of many possibilities deep within us! And whoever believes enough in him can move forward without fear, and this is the starting point of our new life.
Learn more to "be" than to "become", and "to be" is to live in the present, awake moment, where the sad past no longer exists, or the future is not yet; Your life is what you make of it right now, it's built there, right away!

I do not know if everyone will have clearly understood the message and who is really our friend in this adventure! I leave it to you to find the answer that is in you, for sure, it will take longer depending on mental conditioning, but with willpower, you will get there just like me.

All the answers are in you! For you to find them !

*With mount is shown*

*Dominant sapphire ruby*

*Blood is shed to him*

*Outside its future*

*Without waiting in the arena*

## Step 12:
## The traveler

*"The traveler must knock on all the doors before reaching his own."*
*(Rabindranàth Tagore / The Lyric Offering)*

*How did this story start? I have a very vague memory of this meeting that changed my life. was that a dream? The whisper of an illusion? My eyes opened in the train car, no longer remembering how I got here.*

*I was on my way to a new destination, that of a captivating adventure. Two hours from Paris, impatient at the idea of meeting the one who awakened me in a new universe, and the fear of the crowd on arrival won me more and more, in this station in a rather tense context, police and soldiers everywhere took me away from my dreams. The awakening was brutal to be.*

*In the same train where protesters sang "We're here ... .. we're here ... ... !! In yellowish parades, ready to beat the pavement in place of Liberty.*

*I can't wait to see my friend, my author, to sign his book "The lead of life".*

*I had time to start a little nap, and what did I have to do in the meantime? I took my coat as a pillow, the book on my knees, it didn't take me long to fall asleep, as if something made me do it, something soporiphic.*

*I had a funny dream, halfway between the real and the imaginary, and I did not know where I was at this moment, a dream that seemed to be endless, and the one where I write these lines with my pen on a draft notebook, and these words that finalize this adventure are:*

*"Never trust appearances!"*

Throughout this adventure, I understood one important thing!

We are all the guardians of our temple, that of our thoughts, no one can enter it without our authorization, because we alone have the key to our soul, and this friend, full of mysteries is a very close being that only subtlety can to distinguish.

But the innocence of childhood has made us manipulable beings under the influence of protagonists that we believed and let go, it is only in adulthood that we keep locked up many characters as quoted in this book .

There is a drawer who draws the lines of our life from our birth, a child, the one who stayed deep inside us, judges who decide for us what is good or not, a creative genius, our friend very present but asleep, A master of passing time, a farmer who leads the flock, who we are, a philosopher who tries by all means to preach the false for the real, a king incapable of managing his kingdom, a magician who is all the time in us and who shows us what is most beautiful, and a sage who gives us all the revelations about ourselves.

But in the end, who have we become? In fact, we are all these characters, they have become "us", because we happen to be a drawer, child, judge, farmer, philosopher, and all the others who shaped our lives, we are them, but also, the author and actor of our own existence.

The title of my book is not a coincidence, and perhaps also, the fact that you read it, something caught your attention, the image, the title, the subtitle or the description , something made you find your identity in this book.

But let's make one final revelation to you, the traveler, it's you, because only you decide which route you want to follow, which quest you want to be the author of.

You have all the characters in your mind to become who you want, it's up to you to fight the judges of your existence and to awaken your creative genius, the one who gave you powers being younger, and the one who still can, only , it is up to you to take back control of the front door of your soul, only you have the key.

\*\*

*Rule n°5*
*The reality is what we make of it!*

\*\*

## *SUGGESTED READINGS*

**ÉDITIONS BOD**

*- GUARANTEED SUCCESS*
*Yoann MERITZA*

*- HOW TO REPROGRAMM YOUR SUBCONSCIOUS MIND ?*
*Yoann MERITZA*

**UN MONDE DIFFERENT**

*- MAXIMUM SUCCESS*
*Max PICCININI*

*- UNLIMITED CONFIDENCE*
*Franck NICOLAS*

*- LAW OF ATTRACTION*
*Michael J. LOSIER*

*- THE SECRET*

*Rhonda BYRNE*

## EDITIONS BELIVEAU

*- 7 ESSENTIAL INGREDIENTS TO MASTER THE LAW OF ATTRACTION*
*Jack CANFIELD - Mark Victor HANSEN - Jeanna GABELLINI - Eva GREGORY*

## POCHE MARABOUT

*- THE COUÉ METHOD*
*Emile COUE*

*- THE POWER OF POSITIVE THINKING*
*Norman Vincent PEAL*

## MACRO EDITIONS

*- YOU ARE BORN RICH*
*Bob PROCTOR*

## EDITIONS FIRST

*- THE LITTLE BOOK OF THE LAW OF*

ATTRACTION
*Slavica BOGDANOV*

**EDITIONS DU TRESOR CACHE**

*- SECRETS OF A MILLIONARY MIND*
*T Harv EKER*

**J'AI LU**

*- THE SECRET CODE OF YOUR DESTINY*
*James HILMAN*

*- COMPLETE YOUR DESTINY*
*Wayne W. DYER*

*- WHEN WE WANT WE CAN !*
*Normann Vincent PEAL*

*- HOW TO SUCCEED YOUR LIFE?*
*Dr Josephe MURPHY*

*- HOW TO USE THE POWER OF YOUR SUBCONSCIOUS MIND ?*
*Dr Joseph MURPHY*

- *THE POWER OF WILL*
*Paul-Clément JAGOT*

- *THE GAME OF LIFE*
*Florence Scovel SHINN*

- *YOUR WORD IS A MAGIC WAND*
*Florence Scovel SHINN*

- *THINK ABOUT AND BECOME RICH*
*Napoleon HILL*

- *THE SECRETS OF COMMUNICATION*
*Richard BANDLER & John GRINDER*

- *BECOME A MENTALIST*
*Bastien BRICOUT*

**LE LIVRE DE POCHE**

- *HOW TO MAKE FRIENDS*
*Dale CARNEGIE*

- *HOW TO SPEAK IN PUBLIC*

*Dale CARNEGIE*

**EDITIONS ASKA**

*- SMARTER THAN THE DEVIL*
*Napoleon HILL*

**- EDITIONS « POUR LES NULS »**

*- THE LAW OF ATTRACTION FOR DUMPS*
*Slavica BOGDANOV*

**EDITIONS ADA**

*- THE SECRETS OF SUCCESS*
*Sandra Anne TAYLOR*

*- ATTRACT WHAT YOU WISH*
*Mélodie FLETCHER*

**EDITIONS BUSSIERE**

*- THE SECRET DOOR LEADING TO SUCCESS*
*Florence Scovel SHINN*